# INDIAN S[

CW00521420

# INDIAN SUMMER

## JUNE MORTON

# ACKNOWLEDGEMENTS

Special thanks go to DAVE for his expertise and sound advice. Imparted over enough large lattes and cappuccinos to strip a coffee plantation of its crop and deplete a dairy of its milk supplies. Due more, I might add, to my limited technological skills, than any failure on the part of my tutor to pass on his wealth of knowledge.

Grateful Thanks also to the YouWriteOn team for a gentle hand on the steering wheel at certain stages of what has proved an epic and somewhat traumatic journey to get this four-part Saga into print.

# DEDICATION

To the memory of Mary Isobel Catherine
Bernadette O'Brien OBE

AKA   DUSTY SPRINFIELD

16/4/39 – 2/3/99

This is a work of fiction. All persons, businesses and incidents in this book are either the product of the author's imagination or used in a fictitious manner. Any resemblance to actual persons, living or dead, is coincidental.

**Part 1**

# CHAPTER 1

SPRING 1980
KENTLEY MANOR   CENTRAL ENGLAND

She was in love. Forty-five and for the first time. not been in the script for Claudia Elliott's conventional, what those outside her immediate circle might be tempted to call a charmed life.

Wrong time. Wrong place. Well…wrong everything.

Charles Elliott slammed shut the fridge.

'Do you have starters prepared? It's gone seven.'

'Say again.' Claudia's head stayed buried in a copy of *Country Living* as Charles glanced for a third time at some jottings pinned to the kitchen notice board.

'What have you done with the starters? I'm looking at your list of menu suggestions for tonight. *Paupiettes of smoked salmon served with dill.* First item. Underlined in red.' He raised his voice to a shout. 'Our guests are due. Pronto.'

A bout of amnesia had joined forces with his wife's part deafness. There was no other explanation Charles could think of, to account for Claudia's latest woolly-headed behavior. He remained unenlightened as to what made her tick. Despite their fourteen years of marriage.

But then, the society wedding had not been a love match. More an avoidance of getting left on the shelf in Claudia's case. Having reached thirty without being so much as turned on, let alone swept off her feet, by Charles or any of her former suitors. Nor them with her. Once they experienced the pandemonium which could erupt at any time, from her refusal to address the hearing issue and seek help.

While for Charles, only son of a neurotic, overprotective mother, and womanizing, oft times absent father, the marriage, even in the light of such drawbacks, had presented itself as a Godsend.

Indeed, on a highly positive note, their shared Christian faith had proved a solid foundation to hold them together as each of their three children came along.

'Yes. I mean no.' Claudia at some length replied, about the meal.

'Yes or no?' Charles bellowed.

She flicked the page of the magazine, tossed back her honey-blonde hair, and looked up.

'Since you've made it your business, no. Waitrose were out of my usual salmon. I'm serving celeriac remoulade instead. Rob suggested I might give it a whirl when we popped out for supper at the.. the...'

Taking off her reading specs, she brandished them in mid-air, as one might upon receiving special insight they had, in a moment of dire need, turned into a magic wand.

'Oh, you know, 'she then went on. With no added marks for pronunciation, but at least a decent measure of aplomb. 'The Jardin d'ete' place. They took us there on your last birthday.'

'Mmm, well, you're the cook.' Charles thought it expedient not to argue. Either concerning the fact they'd just docked in Cadiz on a Med cruise, the day his forty seventh birthday dawned, or about the revised meal plan.

'Yes quite,' she replied, putting down the magazine. 'I asked their chef for his recipe before we left. In my best French, of course.'

She spoke not a word of French, as far as Charles knew. A theory borne out by her inability to pronounce the name of the restaurant where she had eaten scores of times when visiting her cousin and his French wife Camille in Provence. Claudia had many talents. But languages were not among them.

She went to turn down the oven and took a few steps towards where Charles was standing. Left hand on hip, the fingers of his right tracing the worry lines written into his forehead.

'Everything is under complete control. Now please would you mind getting out of the kitchen?'

Charles would have been glad to. But before there was chance came a head-to-toe inspection.

'Then you might get changed for a start. What are you doing in that ghastly attire?'

At this Charles finally headed for the stairs. Muttering to himself all way up to one of five bedrooms, leading off a large gallery landing of the new build home they'd agreed to call Parklands.

It was a Thursday evening with only a week to go before Easter. Charles had left his exec post with Central Rail in the hands of his deputy and caught an early train, before hastening to shower and pour himself into a size too small, off the peg little number. A puce colored jacket, along with a pastel pink shirt and a pair of ill-fitting flannels, having come to his attention being hauled from two huge carriers Claudia had done battle with to get through the front door. Throwing the items over the back of the sofa, she had sunk down into it, declaring the outfit an absolute snip. 'Just the ticket' she had said, for when they did one of their spots of entertaining.

With hubby dispatched. Eager to get into something less likely to result in long term damage to both his manhood and his reputation, Claudia went to deal with the overlooked starters. Anxious for time alone to collect her thoughts.

Truth to tell, she had been nowhere near Waitrose, nor Kentley's impressive new shopping mall. Beyond doubt, she would zoom down there most days, on her trusty, top of the range scooter. A routine established the minute their move to the town's northern outskirts was complete. With the beloved scooter her means of transport. Ever since, having failed her driving test four times, she'd sailed through the motorcycle one first attempt. And that day, it had been business as usual. She'd been heading into town. Until instinct had prompted her to pull on her brakes as she approached Bentley Common and St Mark's Rectory where Reverend Simon Barclay and his wife Vivienne lived.

After spotting Viv Barclay, Claudia had done an immediate detour. Up to the rectory's front gates, and onto the gravel drive sweeping all way round the large Edwardian building.

10

'Ah, perfect timing. I've just put the kettle on.'

The rector's wife had seen Claudia whipping off her helmet as she was heading indoors. Arms piled high with school shirts and blouses, sports kit, odd socks by the dozen. Everything teenagers wear and need frequent washing had dried nicely in the spring sunshine. The clergy couple had been blessed with a sizeable family. Notwithstanding Mrs. Barclay's self-confessed preference to those whom she trusted, for relations with her own sex. Vivienne Jayne Barclay was quite a woman and, once having ditched the washing so she could greet her guest with open arms, the softness and warmth of her embrace sent Claudia's heart, already thumping from the effort of propping the machine on its stand, into overdrive. By then it was thumping so loud she felt convinced Viv would hear it.

She put the helmet on the scooter seat and took a pile of old *Country Livings* and two *She* magazines from its front basket. Left there for the kind of opportune moment this one had turned into.

'Thought I'd drop by with these, since I was passing.'

Viv took the lot and leading Claudia in by the side entrance, went to put the magazines in the reading room rack.

'Those will be a good excuse for putting my feet up,' she remarked, returning to the hallway where Claudia was wrestling her way out of a burnt orange color padded jacket.

'*You* put your feet up,' she countered.

'Yes. But don't ask me when.' Viv replied with a sigh.

Minutes later was to find the women sitting facing one another on two breakfast benches either side of a long pinewood table in the rectory's bright airy kitchen, overlooking the back lawn and small orchard beyond. Where Claudia, once refreshed from her brew, could have felt at ease for a while to enjoy the conviviality of her surroundings. Had it not been for a bothersome tremor affecting both her hands which, despite her inbred sense of propriety, left her wishing she had been given a mug. So the repeated clink of the China cup against its saucer would not have provided evidence of the state she was getting herself into.

As things were, it had not escaped the Barclay woman's notice. One jot.

The Elliott wife could often be spotted bustling about the place after the Barclays took her on for a bit of additional help. This had come about when Claudia called by with a Victoria sponge and one of her paintings. Her way of getting to know folks who, like them, were still settling in. And that was how it began. The pure joy which would bubble up to cause her heart to skip a beat, accompanied by a supersonic lift in her spirit. The moment Vivienne was near.

Claudia went to put her empty cup on a side of the sink's double drainer. The aroma of fresh spring flowers filled the air. She followed the trail of their scent. A bundle of hyacinths, sprays of jonquil and an assortment of tulips took little finding, waiting to be rescued from their abandonment at a far corner of the worktop. She fetched a gaily painted porcelain vase, relieving it of abject redundancy,

12

save adding a splash of color to a shelf, then went to the sink and filled the vase with water.

'Oh, bless you,' Viv remarked, getting up to go load the dishwasher while Claudia went in search of something with which to trim the blooms.

'Debbie, the flower lady breezed through with that lot first thing,' Viv remarked, upon Claudia's return from the potting shed with a pair of secateurs. 'End of day batch going for a song at the wholesalers according to Debs,' the rector's wife continued. 'They'd just slipped my mind by the time I'd done making sure our absent-minded crew didn't leave everything including their heads behind in the usual scramble to leave the house on time.'

Claudia was grateful to Debbie for responding to the offer and for the chance it gave her to linger. Toiling happily, as was becoming the norm. Outside her agreed hours without extra pay. And the reason the shopping trip had gone on hold.

All she'd needed to do was pop into the splendidly stocked new freezer store, to rustle up something impressive for their guests. Claudia was a dab hand in that situation.

In the one she faced here though her experience was zilch. And the tension around the kitchen table was electric when Claudia, having managed to occupy herself with the task in hand, became aware of Viv's presence. At close enough range, too, to arouse in her more curious stirrings. Of a truly delectable kind.

For Viv Barclay, however, decision time had arrived. With her lips grazing Claudia's left ear, it being the better of the two, and with Claudia already drowning in a sea of delight, Viv placed one hand either side of her trim waist.

'You've got the hots for me. Haven't you my darling?' She spoke in little more than a whisper. Yet, as the words left her lips, Viv knew she must step back. Or let the chemistry raging between them have its way.

She went to sit down and with arms outstretched on the table, made them the focus of her gaze.

'What I'm trying to say,' she began with Claudia still doing her best to complete the arrangement, 'this… well, this *thing* that has developed so quickly between you and I. It cannot take its course. Not here. Not anywhere.'

Lifting her eyes to look across the table, the rector's wife went on, 'All our lives ruined in an instant. If even a whisper of what you and I had been up to, found its way around the parish.'

No stranger to such crises of conscience, Viv Barclay had, on occasions, given in to the dictates of her own need. Although never so close to home. Here, on her husband's patch, they were simply the parish priest and his wife. Called to serve the needs of Simon's congregation. Always on hand as required.

The women stood around equal height. The rector's wife, in her high black stilettos worn to complement a figure-hugging purple/black fleck wool skirt, was an inch or two above average.

'We can't start anything. We absolutely cannot.' She repeated, mantra fashion, her admonition, before getting up to saunter round to where Claudia, by some miracle of grace, was putting the finishing touches to her arrangement.

As she turned, Viv was right there.

'Oh, they'll cheer the sitting room up no end,' she exclaimed, inhaling their fragrance. As instinct took her another step in Claudia's direction. 'You are mightily clever I have to say,' she gushed, adding, 'In so many ways, too.' Reaching out, she touched Claudia's forearm where the sleeves of her cotton blouse had been rolled back at the start of her task. Her hands shot behind her now and she clutched the edge of the wooden table. Afraid her legs might give way.

And it was then Viv thought she would not resist an overwhelming impulse to kiss her. To kiss that generous mouth with its full rounded lips. Now parted inviting delivery. It took every ounce of her will not to take hold of Claudia right there and then. To enfold her in an embrace more meaningful than she, herself, had ever experienced. An action from which she knew, if carried through, there would be no turning back.

The hall clock striking four was to prove her instrument of rescue. Simon was not due home until evening. But their two girls would be flying through the rectory's front door any minute. And, whether Josh, their youngest had stayed behind for his beloved football practice, or not, Jeremy would be pounding through from college.

'That looks yummy mummy. Count me in for dinner,' having been Jez's parting shot, at catching sight of the huge hotpot his mother had been preparing for Molly, the housekeeper, to pop in the oven later.

With this image filling her mind, Viv stepped back. Nearly tripping over the ironing board as she did so. A reminder of her good intentions when Claudia had arrived on the scene.

She checked her watch against the hall clock.

'Golly, it really *is* turned four. So, look. I'm *enormously* thankful for your time and all you've done. But would you mind awfully leaving? I've the dickens of a journey in the morning.'

She picked up the ironing board to take to the laundry room and to collect the abandoned washing. 'Mummy's gone into hospital,' she continued. Upon her return, while proceeding to fold the clean items. 'They're right down in Westport, so I'm going to be away all weekend.'

The promise to go help her parents had been a half one. 'If I can fit things in around my terribly tight schedule,' Viv had explained to her father on the phone. All the while hoping her younger sister would take a fair share of the responsibility. Seeing she lived nearer.

Claudia, however, was not privy to the matter. And the way things were looking, the rector's wife had concluded, by the time all she could hear was the roar of a motor scooter competing with the din only end of term students can make, it was the perfect opportunity to let this entire business calm down. Until she summoned the strength and the courage to do what she knew she truly must.

Not only for the sake of her and her love-struck admirer. But for the benefit of them all.

# CHAPTER 2

'Well, I must say this duck's done to perfection. Never tasted anything so succulent and tender. Compliments, as ever, go to the chef.' James Parker-Snell raised a glass, filled to the brim with his favorite Chablis. 'You never cease to please, Claudia. Or to amaze me with your talents.'

Madeleine Parker-Snell put down her knife and fork.

'I agree. This sauce could not be more flavorsome if you had gone all the way to Seville and picked the oranges. And the bird simply has to be Gressingham. So, don't try convincing me otherwise. In fact, it would be no surprise if you were to announce you'd zipped all the way over to your Uncle Tom's Norfolk farm to ensure freshness.' Maddie dabbed, daintily, at one corner of her mouth with a napkin. 'You put me to shame Claudia. You really do. Although, I have to say when contact with our darling son verges on non-existent, we can guarantee to lure him back into the fold with an offer of his mama's lamb ragout. Provided it comes with a huge mountain of buttery mash.'

'Ah, Peregrine. He's at Warwick, of course.' Claudia took a sip of her wine. 'Settled in, I take it. Must be. If you hear nothing.'

'Oh. Heard nothing for weeks on end after Christmas. Did we Jim?'

'Nope. Not a peep' Jim replied before Maddie took up the conversation again.

'Not till I dropped him a note, reminding him of his papa's birthday and the promise of mammoth helpings of his favorite dish if he would care to come home.'

'Ah, not so good then. He's come home. Poor Peregrine. Such a bright boy as well.'

'No, not permanent. It was just a visit for his dear papa's..'

'Look. Say no more Maddie. No need for explanations. You're among friends. He'll find his niche. Don't you worry.'

Charles was busy re-filling everyone's glass. Maddie made a halt sign with her right hand.

'Not for me Charles. I've drawn the short straw for the drive home.' She gazed across the table at Claudia. Best move the conversation on from Peregrine, she thought. Steer away from that muddle. If she had to speak any louder though, she would be hoarse by the end of the evening.

Scratching around for a suitable topic, Maddie considered asking how Claudia was getting on at art class. Then thought better of it. Upon recalling how they hadn't arrived home until the early hours after one notably long visit. Not so bad. Claudia's paintings were splendid. A joy to behold. If only there was the chance to ask a question or two and get a sensible answer. But there never was. Maybe a show of interest in her trips to the Cotswolds sprang to mind next. Before Maddie talked herself out of that one. She had never been able to keep a straight face at the thought of her friend roaring around the finer parts of quintessential England in a crash helmet on a high-powered scooter. How she had never come a cropper with her hearing, or rather, lack of, Maddie couldn't work out. She settled on reciprocal family news as the safest bet in the end. Having overheard Carolyn, immediately upon their arrival, speaking of someone in the household having taken on work at the rectory.

'Now, do tell. How are your three doing? If I understand correctly, Carolyn has got herself a little job at the rectory. For the Easter hols, I expect. Sensible girl. Earn herself..'

'Yes that's right.' Charles thought it high time he chipped in.

'No. Not Carolyn. I am the one who's taken a job.'

Claudia raised her voice above and, in synchronization with that of Charles.

Confusion reigned.

Charles shot Claudia one of his, `don't you dare say another word` looks. They were just about finished with the mains. James looked quizzically across to where Charles was pouring himself more wine. Maddie caught hubby's eye, then glanced from Claudia to Charles. This was getting out of hand. Too much like hard work. Her attention returned to Claudia who was clearing away the plates. As she headed for the kitchen Charles touched his right ear and spoke again.

'It's getting worse.' He got up. 'Do excuse me. Here. Have some more wine.' He tossed Jim the corkscrew to open the next bottle, waiting on the table on ice, then followed hot on his wife's heels. She was piling the used crockery on the worktop. He put his lips to her left ear.

'Now listen. What in heaven's name is the point of letting those two, of all people, know our business? And that you're doing all these stints, shifts, or whatever it is you're up to, and God alone knows, at the rectory.' Charles lifted the lid to put the empty wine bottle in the bin. He did a double take. 'And what …what the blazers is this?' His eyes had lighted on some cellophane wrap. He pushed the dining room door to and held up the sticky exhibit which clear as crystal, bore the label *'Iceland Super Saver Range. Oven Ready Duck a l'Orange'.*

Charles scratched the top of his head where his hair was fast receding. He stuffed the wrapping out of sight and gave his hands a good wash under the kitchen tap.

'Claudia. Claudie. Now look. This is getting past a joke. Since when did we?'…

'Oh, for goodness' sake. Norfolk. Iceland. Oven ready. Or still half-frozen. What's the difference? You heard the comments. If there is one place I cannot put a foot wrong, it's here.' Taking a serving spoon, she rapped it with great enthusiasm upon the worktop, to mark out her territory which comprised the entire country kitchen.

'Sssh,' Charles hissed and responded with a glare.

Claudia glared back.

'No. I won't sssh. Just make yourself useful by asking if they would like the raspberry roulade or the Eton mess. Then go make conversation. You and I sure do need a natter. But *not* now.'

Charles went away and returned with the orders. One raspberry roulade, one Eton mess and nothing for him, thank you, except a strong coffee. He needed to restore clarity of mind, to gloss over another kind of mess which had once been their marriage.

Having checked for evidence of where the dessert options had been sourced, on finding none, he went to sit down.

James got up and popped his head into the kitchen.

'No need to hurry. We could do with a breather. We're a bit on the full side, m'dear.'

'Quite right Jim. I quit worrying long since. It *is* wonderful, as you say, that I can hear. And without that stupid device Charles insists I mess with. I detest it.'

Jim gave up and went to sit down. Intrigued by what was going on at the table.

'The fact is Claudia, my Claudie, bless her heart, has undergone a kind of spiritual transformation.'

Charles attempted to explain.

'Well, I mean. We have our beliefs. Baptized and confirmed into the Church of England. Both of us. But this latest business is quite something else. It's beyond me.'

What more could he say to folks they would not hesitate to name among their closest friends. They had moved several notches up the housing ladder after Charles's hard-fought promotion. And now Claudia had taken on work at the rectory. A glorified cleaner from what he could make out. For a pittance.

'Ah-ha.' Maddie spoke next, an air of wisdom settling upon her. She checked for signs of Claudia's re-appearing before carrying on. 'She does have a certain glow about her. I've been thinking so all evening.'

'Mmm, can't say I'd noticed,' Charles replied. 'All she's willing to divulge and then, only when pressed, is that it's part of what she describes as her reasonable service as a born-again believer.'

'Oh, my good gracious. She's joined the happy clappies.' Jim had put his finger right on it, he was sure, then became lost in thought. He stroked what remained of his goatee beard after the severe treatment it had received at the hands of his wife in preparation for their social evening. 'Although I would never have thought Claudia the type.' He turned to Maddie. 'Well, would you, dear?'

Maddie shrugged. Two-thirds of a glass of anything stronger than lemonade shandy and she could be persuaded the Pope was the new Dalai Lama.

'Yes, but they're not.' Charles re-joined the conversation. 'They're not happy anything down there. That's what baffles me. I go with her most Sundays. Nothing out of the ordinary to report. Could be any Anglican church we'd walked into.'

'Hormones then Chas. If you ask me.' Maddie gave the matter her best and final guess. She'd just turned fifty and knew what she was talking about. Having astounded herself and horrified their daughter by embarking on a fling with the man who came to lay new carpets.

Annunciata, or Nunnie, as she was known among her friends had caught her mother and the carpet man in a compromising situation. There was no way, at fifteen, she could be convinced it was standard practice to lie down in one's underwear to test the quality of the pile, before the tradesman left the premises.

Maddie was not particularly religious. But had gone to church six Sundays in a row, to secure pardon and give thanks her Jim hadn't found out. Nunnie having been sworn to secrecy with the promise of a weekend away at a top spa resort. Paid for out of the discount her mother had secured on the carpets.

Was Claudia undergoing a similar, out of character thing? She was, when all was said and done, coming up to forty-six.

Maddie spoke again, pulling no punches and looking Charles in the eye.

'Mid-life crisis looming I reckon then, Chas. You're going to need oodles of.. '

With no time for further speculation, Claudia flounced in.

'Here we are. Now who's for raspberry roulade?'

James raised a finger while Maddie prepared to do justice to the Eton mess.

Claudia pushed a small helping of the roulade around her plate and glanced at her watch. Was that the time? Quarter to ten. And was that hint of mischief in hubby's eye one she couldn't fail to recognize? The coffee had sobered him. He appeared to have forgotten their exchanges in the kitchen. Forgiven her. Whatever there was to forgive. Three glasses of Chablis and Charles Elliott was as amorous as he ever got. And tonight, Claudia reasoned, may prove no exception.

There followed several minutes of amiable silence while James and Maddie sipped their coffees. Claudia added cold milk to hers and quickly downed it, then collecting the dessert plates, disappeared back into the kitchen.

James stretched and gave a yawn.
'Oh, excuse me folks. I'm sleepy. But thanks again Chas for such unprecedented hospitality. And to your darling wife for filling us with food fit for a king.' He gave Maddie a discreet dig in the ribs, detecting she was about to nod off. Drained by her attempts at marriage guidance. 'What say you, dearie?'

Maddie gave a startled jolt.

'Oh! And a queen. Absolutely.' She got up and staggered to the kitchen with their dirty cups.

Claudia was taking her time loading the dishwasher. She needed a moment. Her intuition was giving due warning. The night was not over.

The three Elliott siblings had long since retreated to their rooms with pizza suppers. With the guests now ready to leave, the women exchanged a hug.

'Do enlighten me *please*, on your activities at St Mark's.' Maddie whispered into Claudia's good ear. Then stepped back to take in her appearance one last time.

'You look splendid on it. And that gown. Well, what can I say?'

Claudia had slipped into a midnight blue halter neck chiffon gown, soon as she'd dealt with the overlooked starter course. Five minutes before their guest's arrival and an hour after Charles had stepped into the safe familiarity of a pair of grey flannels and the sheer comfort of a white, open neck shirt.

'Oh, thank you.' Claudia exclaimed, in reply to Maddie's compliment. 'I ran it up only last week to try out the new Elna Club I snapped up in Lewis's sale.'

'My. Your talents, as well as your unique ability to sniff out a bargain know no bounds.' Maddie went on before airing her final suggestion. 'I think a girlie get together is in order, the minute you're not *quite* so occupied.' With right hand covering one side of her mouth, she continued 'At the rectory.'

Claudia remained silent as the two men bid each other goodnight.

'See you for a few rounds at the club old boy when you have some vacation.'

Jim gave Charles a hearty slap on the back.

'Not so much of that. You old codger you. I'm nowhere near my half century yet.' Charles had the last word as the Elliott's waved.

Just as the Parker-Snell's got into their XJ6 and with Madeleine at the wheel, off they sped.

# CHAPTER 3

'Charles. *Please*. I'm so tired.'

Claudia resisted her husband's first tentative grope. The moment the light was out and as she was about to enter another dream filled slumber. More of the kind any teenager might experience, than of a woman approaching her middle years.

Charles continued his quest. A bit of gentle lovemaking could only soothe her tiredness and lift her mood. To his way of thinking, anyhow.

'It's been a splendid evening. Always is when we have Jim and Maddie round.'

Claudia lay stock still on her right side as she felt his hand slip inside the top section of her nightie.

'We all sing from the same hymn sheet. That's for sure.' Charles went on. The hand, having reached its goal, beginning to fondle her breast. 'Especially if we disregard one or two, shall we say hiccups, at the table tonight?'

Every nerve in Claudia's body became on edge.

'Reminds me how close we came to going all the way.'

As the trip down memory lane continued, the caressing and fondling gathered pace.

'That weekend we spent with them in the Wye Valley. Just before the big day.'

Claudia inwardly flinched as he reached right over to give the other breast equal share of attention.

'It's the nearest you and I ever got to real passion.'

She outwardly flinched as the activity intensified, to the accompaniment of more reminiscing. But he failed to notice.

'That last night, we found ourselves alone and you let me slip your panties off...'

She couldn't take any more. The thin cotton nightie afforded little protection from the growing evidence of her husband's need for what she could no longer freely give. She turned onto her back and flicked on a small light above the headboard.

'Look, Chas. It's late and I'm not in the mood for what you have in mind. I've told you, I'm exhausted. All that running around. As well as having to make small talk.' She pulled the lower part of the three-quarter length nightie down, far as it would go and did up the top buttons.

'I find Maddie draining these days, to be honest,' she remarked, relaxing slightly.

It was time for Charles to question his own hearing.

'*You* find *Maddie* draining. Excuse me.'

'Yes, I do. And never mind the excuse me's. Just get rid of the blessed hiccups.'

'Hiccups?'

'Yes. Hold your breath or something. Don't pretend it's my hearing. I heard perfectly. You said you had hiccups.'

'Ah. The hiccup at the table is what I was getting at.'

Oh, good grief. This was more than a passion killer, Charles reflected. This was enough to bring on a breakdown.

'Well, if it was at the table, serves you right. Drinking all that wine. Gulping it down you were. And why mention it now? Really Chas. Sometimes I can't make you out.'

Well, my, oh jolly well, my! If Maddie's suspicions were correct, if this turned out to be the menopause and only the start, he would be putting in for an overseas posting. The sort which came up on the international rail bulletin now and then.

These and similarly desperate thoughts were racing through Charles's mind as Claudia ventured to face him.

'Anyhow, seeing we are both wide awake,' she began, there's something I feel the need to share.'

With her gaze now directed now toward the ceiling, Charles rolled onto his back. He should have read the signals more accurately. That was obvious. Claudia had turned away from him, soon as he'd switched out the light. Not a position anyone intent upon seducing their partner would take up, the minute they were alone and in bed. He gave a deep sigh. His spoiled night of love paling into insignificance at the prospect of what lay ahead. A full-on life changing crisis. Of gigantic proportions. By the look of things.

He rubbed his now extremely tired eyes.

'What is it? I can catch the seven thirty in the morning instead of the six forty. It will give balance to the day ahead, I suppose.' He yawned and gave another sigh. 'I've a meeting late tomorrow afternoon.'

Charles's amorous intentions took another dip as his thoughts turned to the emergency briefing between the London Met and the rail network's Design and Safety department. A man had died after falling or been pushed from a train. The weariness reflected in his voice when he spoke again.

'Spill the beans. Then perhaps we'll both get some rest.'

If it's more items from that sprawling home furnishings department she spends most of her time in when not at the rectory, Charles began to speculate, where on earth is she thinking of putting them? What could she have her eye on now? Carpets became his final inspiration, upon recalling her disenchantment with those laid when they moved into Parklands. Coupled with Jim's tale of how they had fitted the whole of their downstairs at an extraordinarily reasonable rate.

Well, that was do-able without adding to the clutter. If it was going to keep her quiet for a while.

Claudia, meantime, was gathering every ounce of her courage.

Dear, kind Charles. She had no wish to hurt him. But things had come to a head.

'Charles. I'm..' She looked his way briefly then shot up a prayer before wading in.

'I'm in love,' she said quietly.

Well, I never, was to be Charles's initial silent reaction. It could be nothing more than his omission of certain whispered endearments which had cost him a romantic interlude with his wife. So, what was the panic? He would do things differently next time. And make what amends he could straight away. He turned to search her misty green, clearly troubled eyes.

'I may not put it into words. But I love you, too. My own sweet Claudie.' He touched her cheek. More tenderly than he had touched her anywhere in years. '*In love* though. That's never been on our agenda. Or has it?' He continued after a pause.

'I thought we'd always agreed, with the faith and other basic ideas we share, we'd get by without much of the slushy sentimental kind of business.'

He shot his wife an anxious glance.

'We both still hold to that. Surely.'

With no immediate response and, regardless of Claudia's predisposition to swing from one bright idea to the next, Charles found himself in need of reassurance.

'Well, don't we?'

This was proving trickier than she had hoped.

'Chas. That is not what I meant. Not *you* and I involved in this equation.'

'I see,' he tentatively remarked. Realizing they were, at last, getting somewhere. Painful as it may be. 'I've always known I wasn't enough for you. We've spoken of that before, too.'

'Oh.'

'Yes. My works dinner. A couple of Christmases ago. You spent the entire evening exchanging funny stories with our chief architect. I remember remarking on the way home, if he happened to be a fellow believer, he could be just your cup of tea.'

Charles response was already bordering on resignation.

'Whilst I realize I can't compete with these..'

'Charles. Will you listen?' Claudia sat bolt upright to find herself peering down at, what had, in that instant become, an expression she'd seldom seen cross her hubby's face. It was of perplexity and pain.

Would *he* listen? That was laughable. But, regardless of the gut-wrenching sensation in the pit of his stomach, he would give it his best shot.

'Go on. I'm all ears,' he declared, staring straight ahead as Claudia drew breath to deliver her blow.

'I'm.. well, what I am trying to say is - I'm in love with another woman.'

There. She had said it. 'I'm sorry. So truly sorry. My world's been turned upside down. I've fallen in love with Vivienne, our new vicar's wife.'

'*Aah.*' Things were clicking into place now. Real fast.

'So that's what's fueled your aspirations to become the most talented Mrs. Mop in town. And why you keep hanging back in church. I wondered what the attraction could be. Staying behind to wash up the crocks after everyone except her and the tidying up team have left.'

There followed a lengthy silence as Charles strove to digest everything and, before turning once again, to search her face.

'How long then?' He finally asked.

'How long what?' Claudia was puzzled. Did he think they had started an affair?

'Well. Exactly how long have you been harboring all this?'

'Oh, long enough,' she replied, daring to look his way for a second. Before focusing her attention, this time, toward the foot of the bed. 'I've fought it. God knows I have.'

'Fought it.' Charles gave a puzzled scowl. 'You've gone a funny way about that.'

'Wh..what do you mean?' She stammered.

'Well. It's hardly rational. Is it? Spending all day around the very place you can't avoid the woman.'

Despite his pain, the confession shed light on certain matters. Such as why the midweek entertaining was so high on the agenda. Claudia was spending large chunks of their weekends at every church event that cropped up.

'Does she... does Vivienne have any idea?' He enquired.

'Yes. No. I don't know.'

She did. But was not prepared to give an answer. Until she'd pondered things some more.

'That figures,' Charles remarked.

'Sorry, I've lost you Chas. I never said a thing about fig - ah, unless you mean is it affecting my financial...'

Was it not typical of her husband to run a cost assessment on how the current dilemma he was now facing, might impact his watertight budget? This being Claudia's impression, before Charles cut in.

'Forget it. Just forget it. But thanks, I guess, for your honesty.'

Claudia's honesty of heart, despite her vagueness of mind, had been one of the things which had always endeared her to him.

There was another pause while Charles sought to process it all.

'What more do you want me to say? Faced with such momentous news.' He finally enquired. 'Congratulations upon your discovery, perhaps. I don't know Claudie. I truly don't. All I know is I'm as exhausted as you, now.'

He gave, what turned, this time, into an enormous yawn, and swung his legs to the floor, realizing he needed a pee. He padded off to the adjoining bathroom, then clambered back into bed and set about pummeling his pillows. Tutting and fiddling around, in response to a sudden urge to re-arrange them. He leaned over to adjust the alarm before looking her way one last time.

'Do you think we can get some rest?' He then queried, adding. 'You wouldn't like me to go to the spare room by any chance? If I can do so at this hour. Without alerting the rest of the household to our disunity.'

'Of *course* not.' Claudia's response was as emphatic as her sigh of relief had been a few minutes earlier. At least things were out in the open. A dose of her husband's sarcasm she could cope with. If it was to be his only reaction.

While, for the moment Charles simply moved out of reach and slid under the covers. Too done in to say another word.

And Claudia, her relief tainted by only the mildest pang of guilt riding on huge waves of excitement, switched off the light and fell, without further trouble, into that overdue, dream filled slumber.

34

# CHAPTER 4

APRIL 1980
ST MARK'S RECTORY BENTLEY COMMON

Trust all is well with mummy and pops. We need to speak <u>soon</u> - will be in 6ish x

The clergy wife screwed up the note and put down her overnight bag with a sigh. She made her way to the kitchen and flicked on the kettle. What had been going on with only one parent in charge all weekend? And wouldn't it be nice if Simon had, for once suggested they go out for dinner, to discuss whatever couldn't wait until she'd settled back in? The freezer was almost empty. She was exhausted. On top of which, it looked as if Molly, like her sister, in the situation of need she had left behind in Westport, had been nowhere near the place.

The thin square boxes, Pizza Perfecto emblazoned across them, piled high next to the bin, told the story. As did the yellow-stained foil trays, matching a handful of marks on the kitchen worktop. Along with the stench of stale curry. Despite her tiredness, Reverend Barclay's wife experienced a tad of remorse. If she hadn't departed with such haste, she would have put on a better show before setting out.

It was developments with Claudia which had thrown things. At least, there should be no repercussions on that score. Having made herself clear before setting out. She hung up her jacket and kicked off her shoes. Gosh how she needed that cuppa, and minutes later, had never been so thankful to sit down with a steaming mug of her favorite brew.

With the caffeine having delivered its fix, she emptied the contents of her bag into the washer, closed the utility room door on its noisy vibrations and went to the cloakroom to freshen up. After which, she collected her sports bag and headed off towards her local health club, to unwind and catch up on some missed workouts.

It was twenty past six when Reverend Barclay popped his head round the dining-room door to find his wife clearing some space on the table while ruminating over what they could eat. Her choice now restricted by, not only the near empty freezer, but by a bout of severe heartburn. Good job it was the end of term, she silently reflected. It meant the whole family had taken off before she got in, to spend a few nights under canvas with the St Mark's youth team.

'*Come on* Poppet. My study, please.' Simon's voice cut into all such thoughts, as he beckoned her with the crook of his finger. 'Yes., that's it. Come along.'

She'd been cast in the role of naughty schoolgirl. What was the matter? Viv winced and put a finger to her breastbone.

'Just give me a mo. I need to...'

'Now, please, Vivienne.'

She'd been about to go find her Rennies. But the rector paced back and forth. The day had left him irritable and drained. He needed his wife's attention quickly.

'I can skip dinner if Molly hasn't left anything. I did pass the time of day with her on my way out, come to think, and she mentioned finishing early because of the school hols before I had to rush. I'd a funeral at eleven.'

The rector crossed the hall and entered his study as Viv headed out of the kitchen to where he was holding the door open for her.

She ducked beneath his arm. 'That's right,' he said, patting her left one.

Viv went to sit down. She was seething.

'Simon. What on earth..?' What had got into him? He hadn't even asked after her parents. Apart from a mention in the note. His mind was clearly elsewhere.

He cut in, giving her no chance to continue.

'I see no point in beating about the bush. It's wonder woman, Claudia. She was round here Friday morning. Doing her thing.'

Every nerve in Viv's body became on edge.

'Oh yes.'

'Yes. She'd been to Greenmount.'

This being the local garden center.

'Came flouncing in, she did, arms overflowing with those geraniums in there.' He pointed towards the conservatory. 'I think that's what they are. If their pungency is anything to go by. She enquired whether you'd gone on your mission and when I replied yes,' he continued, 'she asked to see me soon as I was free.'

'Oh. Not getting tired of the little job already. Is she? She does strike me as the restless kind.'

Vivienne was hoping Claudia had decided to quit. Taking matters out of her hands.

'No. Not a bit of it.' No such good fortune was running through the rector's mind as he went on.

'I told her I'd a full schedule which I jolly well had. Well, that did it.' He threw up his hands. 'She sat herself there.' He pointed to the chair next to the one his wife was sitting on and began his impersonation.

*'Then Simon, I'll get straight to the point. That way, we all know where we stand.'*

Oh no. Viv inwardly groaned.

She stood up. 'Simon, I can ex..'

He cut back in.

'Just let me finish, please. Yes, I expect you know what I'm going to say. I was about to suggest she come back this evening. But the poor, tortured soul couldn't contain herself that long. She's very excitable, this latest one. Isn't she? And prone to the kind of dramatics worthy of winning her an Oscar.'

The mimicry continued. *"I'm in love with your wife. I've tried to deny it. But I can't."* Then she had the audacity to ask if I could recommend suitable counselling.' Looking his wife straight in the eye, he continued. 'Now, I'm telling you Vivienne. It's *not on*. What've you been up to? Again. We've been round this mountain *so* many times.' He wagged a finger. 'Listen. Can you please keep these dalliances of yours outside of my parish? It's the least you can do. For God's sake. Yes, I mean literally. For God's sake.' He took a deep breath and ran his hand through a mop of untidy blonde hair.

'NIMBY, Vivienne. Do you hear? NIMBY.'
'*What?*'

'Not in my back yard, poppet. That's what. If you insist on having these ridiculous... Oh, God help me. If you insist on having these *flings*, would you do me the favor of keeping them away from our doorstep?'

In demonstration of this final point, the rector threw his arms forward in a gesture consistent with one of shooing off a cat using the front lawn as its toilet.

'We may have to curtail your latest ardent and *clearly* lovesick admirer's employment. Sadly.'

'Simon darling. Please. Calm down.'

'No. I mean it. I don't dispute the woman's been an asset. Adding a touch of her own brand of genius around here. That means nothing though. If my reputation *and* yours end up laid on the line. Cool it, is what I'm basically saying. Deal with it. Promptly. Otherwise, I'll have no option but to sack her. There's no contract involved. She's just casual labor. Speak to her please. That's all. Case closed.'

The minister, having stayed on his feet throughout, gave a huge sigh.

'It hasn't been the best of days. God knows it hasn't. Poor fellow whose funeral I was called upon to conduct. Only mid-forties. Another with cancer where no man wants to believe it can get him. Diagnosed too late. Left a wife and two kids.'

He took hold of Viv by the shoulders and kissed the top of her head, towering above her as she faced him. Reverend Barclay was still in love with his wife. Despite what was, as far as he was concerned, her unacceptable behavior.

His voice became husky as he drew her towards him.

'The only thing worth adding is that maybe, my sweet, just maybe *I'm* overdue for a rigorous inspection of my own.'

Viv froze as he drew her closer and with the entire length of his body pressed up against hers, went on. 'And to this end, my precious, perhaps you wouldn't say no to an early night.' His breath became hot on her neck. 'Could be exactly what's needed to raise our spirits.' His intense blue eyes now alight with desire began to search hers. Cradling her face between silken smooth hands, he went on. '*Then* and only then, Mrs. Barclay, might I receive the reassurance I would like, as to where your true romantic inclinations lie.'

He released her.

'Give it some thought, anyhow. While I go jump in the shower.' He remarked. Pausing reflectively for a final moment.

'I'll soon take your mind off your empty tummy. And all else that's troubling you.' At which point the rector strode out of the study. As his long legs mounted the stairs two at a time, he was no nearer resolving this tiresome dilemma. But was prepared to content himself in the short term with the idea of what had, God willing, found its way to the top of his evening's agenda.

Minutes later, in their marital quarters, his wife heard, along with the gush of running water, her husband singing softly in the shower.

When he emerged, she was in bed. And, with whatever it took she was waiting. Having rifled her handbag for the Rennies, she'd taken two then grabbed a handful of crackers. Before putting a block on her innermost feelings. It was time for a spot of role play. Of that fact alone, was she certain. So, despite not an ounce of the spontaneous desire which had threatened to overtake her downstairs so recently with Claudia, she would lie back and with good grace, endure things. For the sake of her husband. And the gratification of his need.

Poor Claudia. Viv mourned her anticipated loss. As the rector partook of his pleasure. And as she realized what she must do the next morning.

My poor, poor darling Claudia was to be her silent lament. Before sinking into several hours of much needed, though mightily troubled sleep.

# CHAPTER 5

A whole year on Claudia could not bear to look back. She would become inconsolable each time her memory played any trick which forced her to recall the thrill, followed by devastation. In those last moments with the Barclay wife.

Vivienne was looking more stunning than ever that fateful morning when Claudia arrived at the rectory. The red tight-fitting sweater and the figure-hugging denims were enough to rocket her into a frenzy of desire. Nine fifteen in the morning, or not. Desire, however, had soon turned to despair.

'Viv. Oh Viv. How good you're still here.'

Ten minutes late due to road works, Claudia had arrived with just one thought. The thought  she was sure to have missed seeing her love. But Viv was still there. And with no sign of anyone else. Had she held back from her day, on purpose? That they might spend time alone.

The rector's wife had been found in the sitting room, perched on the edge of the sofa. Claudia had taken off her scooter jacket and flinging it over an armchair, sat down next to her. Close as possible. Until their thighs were touching, sending bolts as those of high voltage electric coursing through both women. This surely could have been their moment. The one she had dreamed of. But alas, not to be.

Viv had shot up from the sofa.

'Look Claudia. What happened. Well, what might have happened if I hadn't gone to help daddy. And before you embarked on your little tete a tete with Simon. Why did you..?'

Claudia had got back to her feet startled. Upon realizing what was to come.

'Don't. Please, *don't* do this Viv. I can't bear it. You know I'm in love with you. Oh, please, *please* God.'

She'd attempted to throw her arms around the rector's wife's neck. But Viv was having none of it. She had freed herself and placed her hands squarely on Claudia's shoulders. Her blue eyes penetrating Claudia's green ones.

'This, this…well, whatever. It's got to stop.' She'd paused before going on. 'Or Simon is going to ask you to leave. I'm sorry. So truly sorry.'

'No. You're *not*. You're not a bit sorry. You've used me. That's what you've done. I see it all now. Offering me work to turn me into your plaything. Thinking you'd amuse yourself for a while. But my response put paid to your little game. Didn't it? And all because you're married to that...' Claudia had pointed to Simon's ordination photo on display, 'to that boring vicar. Just look at me.'

She had been shaking, rooted to the spot, tears coursing down her cheeks, plopping on to the mahogany wood coffee table. 'Have a heart, Vivienne Barclay. Have you never been in love? Oh, my dear God.' With hands raised high, Claudia's gaze had gone up to the ceiling. 'Please, please Lord, help me. Why has this happened? And what am I going to *do*?'

43

Viv had recalled her husband's remark on Claudia's potential for a career in dramatics. That, at least, had been spot on, she reflected, striving to keep her cool.

'Look my love calm down. There there.' She had put out a hand to stroke her hair before the distraught Claudia had slumped back on the sofa, sobbing.

Viv had, nevertheless, persevered. 'Oh, come along. Nothing's that bad.' She'd got up and gone to the kitchen.

'Just let me make you a nice strong cuppa.' The old English standby of tea and comfort being all, when the chips were down, Viv knew, for certain, she could offer. 'Then things will look up,' she continued. Thinking she would have laced the tea with brandy. Had she known where Simon hid it. The minister being partial to a tipple to sooth his frayed nerves, ever since his days with the airlines. The transition from cockpit to pulpit was a long and sorry tale which had begun with a nervous breakdown. Suffice to say here, it was not one his wife had welcomed with open arms.

After mopping up the tears, Viv had offered Claudia the box of tissues. Ignoring them, Claudia had continued to wail.

'Oh, my Lord. My Good God. What am I going to do? What *am* I going to do?' Bent double, she had folded her arms across her stomach and fixed her eyes on the carpet. The Almighty, it appeared, at one point, had transferred His Presence from the rectory ceiling, to look up and listen from under the floorboards.

Viv had let the wailing continue, whereupon returning from the kitchen with the tea tray, silence had finally descended. A silence the rector's wife had tried to fill with hope.

'Listen. I know how *utterly* painful this is for you. Well, for both of us,' Viv had begun. 'So, I hope you won't yell at my suggestion.'

Seating herself in an armchair opposite Claudia, she had continued. 'Have you, by any chance, heard of the Three F's?'

'What? I can't hear a word.'

Having caught her attention Viv had gone on. 'Three F's. Three F's Plus. To give it its full title. Standing for Females, Fun, Friendship. '*And* more.'

Painful as it had been, to so much as hint at a solution intended to steer her admirer's attention elsewhere, there was no other way out. Viv Barclay had been given no choice, this time, but to sweep her feelings aside. She'd therefore pressed on while Claudia gazed blankly at the tea.

'I realize it may not appeal right now. But do give it thought.' Viv had continued. 'It's a women's friendship.. well, a nicely run women's dating service. There *are* other married women out there, you know. And not all their husbands are vicars.'

Claudia, in that moment, could not have cared less. But the Barclay wife felt she had done her bit.

'Leave me. Wherever you are meant to be. Just go.' Claudia had yelled. 'Before *I* leave. And before you never, *ever* see me, or Charles, or the children again.'

The clergy wife, at that moment, could have envisaged many worse fates which might have befallen her. It had become clear, however, her priority was to allow Claudia time and space to get herself together. And to that end, had slipped quietly away on her bicycle. Being the fine sunny day, it had been. And one, upon which she had never felt more in need of fresh air.

Oh, Good Lord. What a mess, had been uppermost in the Barclay wife's mind as she pedaled alongside the canal. Knowing not where she was heading. A gap in her diary had granted her two hours of grace, in which to process the morning's events.

She had finally braked to a halt outside *The Revived Rose Travelers' Inn*. After spotting the chalked message on their display board telling her **Coffee was being served**, it was an invitation she had been unable to resist. So had dismounted, then chained up her bike. And though something she had never in life, done on her own, she'd wandered in. The board's invitation being a potential sign from the divine, telling her she should.

Whatever the case and with or without heaven's bidding, Viv Barclay had on that day, been one English rose who was in desperate need of reviving.

# CHAPTER 6

'You're pathetic. *Just* pathetic.'

It was several months into Claudia's Three F's membership, and she was only now, on her first date. She no longer went near St Mark's, having given Simon her resignation within days of that rectory scene with his wife. Then, with grief subsiding Claudia had told herself life must go on. So, here she was, standing in a hotel car park with one whom it had taken only the briefest of exchanges over lunch for her date to earn, in Claudia's book, the title of extremely rude character. At the end of a long scooter ride, too.

'What *do* you mean? How dare you?' She was already donning her helmet as the other woman spewed forth her disdain.

''Avin' yer 'usband lookin' after yew. Knowin' yer bleedin' gay. For fucks sake, ger a job an' leave 'im.'

Claudia's face had turned the color of an over ripe plum. Whereupon recovering her composure, there came a moment of perfect hearing.

'The situation I find myself in is not his fault. Nor is it mine or that of anyone else. On top of which I find the entire tone of your conversation vulgar. So please, take yourself and your *filthy* language elsewhere. Goodbye.' After which Claudia had revved up her machine and departed.

It had been clear from the outset the woman was never going to fill Viv Barclay's shoes. There had been a certain appeal though. The floral print button through dress tied round the waist with a broad sash highlighting a sylph like figure had, at least, gained her approval.

Pity, Claudia had got round to thinking as she sped off. If this imbecile had not entertained such harebrained ideas as the one that she should leave Charles, couched in language she'd come across no more than twice on late night TV, they could have enjoyed a liaison of sorts.

It was not meant to be, she had in the end, consoled herself. While back home the Elliott couple continued to share the marital bed. All attempts at intimacy having been curtailed, however, following one traumatic occasion when, at the height of Charles's pleasure, his wife had passed out. Quite mercifully, it had taken only a good shake of the shoulders to return Claudia to the land of the living. But that had been *that*. Their marriage, henceforth, had become one of staunch commitment and amiable friendship. More amiable, it is worth adding, than any pact Claudia had yet forged with her Heavenly Father. The result being a refusal to participate in any act of public worship. Until The Almighty provided a far better solution to her pleas for help in that rectory sitting room than anything He had come up with, thus far.

And Charles, having considered his options, had been quick to recount plenty worse misfortunes that might have crossed his path. Particularly, if one factored in the benefit of no more excuses required to skip church coupled with the perfect opportunity for a morning on the golf course.

Claudia's diary entries of disaster would not be complete without the inclusion of two others which stood out for all the wrong reasons. If a list of incompatibility ratings was to be compiled, then the *Smart Alec seeking bright spark to set her alight*, who turned up in tracksuit and dirty trainers, would have topped it.

The two women had experienced little more than an exchange of greeting on the station concourse when, with due credit to the railways, both parties had arrived bang on time. That, sadly, had proved the highlight. After which it had all gone downhill.

The woman, having recognised Claudia from the photo accompanying her profile, had wasted not a minute in holding out a hand of greeting.

'Clawdiya I prisoom.'

'Resume? What's there to resume?' Claudia had begun.

'No. I said pres...'

'Oh, look.' She had cut in. 'No need to apologize or to explain. The problem, along with your appalling presentation is your dialect. So, if you will excuse me, I have a train to catch. If you cannot dress decently for a first meeting, why bother to turn up at all?' Claudia had not been about to withstand any nonsense.

'I just thawt...'

'Please now, don't exert yourself thinking.' The woman was stopped mid flow as with a haughty sniff and her gaze cast heavenward, Claudia had turned tail into the station. How fortunate she had left her scooter at home in favor of the use of her free rail pass; a perk enjoyed through Charles's job, being her chief reflection as she waited for the train. Otherwise, the mood she was in, and with one speeding fine only recently paid, she might well have incurred another.

One final prospect Claudia could not dismiss from her mind was a forty something year old. Like herself married; she had stated so in her ad. That, along with the *'Cultured Pearl seeking to climb back into her Oyster'* having been the bait to reel Claudia in. Not averse to a little culture herself, Claudia had suggested the two meet at a nearby National Trust venue where an open-air concert was due to be held. The idea of two cultured ladies becoming better acquainted in such a romantic setting filled Claudia with delight. She had therefore gone the extra mile with this one. Since on paper she had shown promise. In the harsh light of day however, she had extracted not a jot of information from the woman inside of ten minutes. Beyond the snippet offered at the outset; this latest unsavory character went by the name of Pearl.

Claudia had waved a leaflet under what she'd been quick to define as Pearl Radcliffe's rather aquiline nose.

'Here we are. Why not join me for this? Four Seasons. Vivaldi. Terrific stuff.'

The woman, with a waft of the hand, had declined both the leaflet and the invite.

'Nah. I'm into rock' had come the reply when she, at last, found her voice. 'Status Quo's my fave.

If it were them or let's say Queen. They're the biz' the woman had gone on, drawing on a long cigarette, eyes fixed to the ground.

'Oh, forget it. Forget we ever met' Claudia had exploded.

She'd about had enough. These women, professional or not, cultured or not, married, single, whatever. Not one came within a country mile of her first love, Vivienne Barclay. Each possessed great drawbacks of some kind. If they didn't smoke like a chimney, they would swear like a trooper or drink like a fish. Most of them surrounding themselves with animals into the bargain. All kinds of creatures Claudia simply couldn't stand. These and several other let downs, too traumatic to begin to describe, she had endured. Till the whole futile business would have driven her to absolute despair.

Had it not been for the company - in which she would find herself... *soon.*

# CHAPTER 7

JUNE 1983
A VERY ENGLISH TOWN AND A FAMOUS
EVENT

'I'll put all my cards on the table. Like you, I'm more years married than I care to count. But would not leave my Karl at any price. He's my rock, my best friend, and the father of my two boys, Jake and Toby. However, I like what I see. The fact I don't share your faith only adds spice to the blend. What say you?'

Before Claudia had time to say a word, her latest date continued. 'I'm a touch creative. Although must confess I can't match you there. But then music's my passion. I teach flute and guitar.' A brief pause ensued. Again, too brief for Claudia to gather her thoughts and respond before the other woman was off again. 'And there's the German class I run with hubby. He hails from Frankfurt you see.' Claudia was about to speak before being beaten a third time. 'Generally, though, I'd say we're cut from the same cloth. Thought so the minute I got your card.'

This member, like the list of also rans had found herself on the receiving end of one of Claudia's finest art creations in the run up to their first meeting.

With breath drawn, Claudia this time managed to chime in. 'You did.'

'Yes.' Bel Janssen replied. Unstinting approval was beginning to register in her facial expression, leading her to continue 'So why don't we give things a try?'

The women were sitting by the river at Henley, sipping their coffees in the afternoon sun, to round off a simple yet satisfying lunch comprising a ploughman's platter they'd agreed to share. All part of an unspoken pact they were not there to fuss about food.

And as things were turning out, this latest candidate whom Claudia hoped against hope would fill the aching void in her heart, was in a league of her own.

Therefore, she sat pondering for no longer than it took to polish off her coffee before she delivered her verdict.

'OK. You're on. We'll give things a try.'

Bel, as she'd introduced herself, even reminded her of Vivienne. Especially in her mannerisms and clear way of speaking. Cambridge graduate too. Perfect, she had instantly decided. Top notch credentials in every department.

Annabelle Janssen was tall. Taller than her. Also slim with shiny shoulder-length chestnut brown hair. She displayed her intellect in a trendy bespectacled fashion. The non-faith aspect didn't trouble Claudia. There would be bags of time for lively discussion. Once they had dealt with the basics.

Why indeed and, regardless of her lingering passion for the rector's wife, Claudia was experiencing *the* most delectable sensations. Beginning in her lower regions and prompting, with some urgency, the enquiry. 'So, where do we go from here?'

Before the words left her lips, Claudia was harboring the hope Bel might suggest she leave her machine in the hotel car park then be driven to the Janssen home in the silver Volvo her date had turned up in. She could always collect her machine later, she had already worked out, then get the train back to their current location. Being only half past two on a midsummer's day, and one upon which she was in no hurry to get home.

'Well.' The other woman began, a note of hesitancy, for the first time in her voice. 'I've a flute lesson this evening and I really ought to get back and give my Karl his dinner. He works mammoth shifts at the car plant. Like your - was it Charles you said?'

'Yes. Chas is an exec with Central Rail.' Claudia replied then went on, 'I hardly see him from one week to the next. When I do, he's bringing work home.'

'Ah, I see.' Bel was forming a picture as she continued 'My Karl's Production Manager at Cowley which, of course, everyone knows of.'

After noting the frequent references to *her* Karl, Claudia gave an affirming nod. Though, in truth, was vague as to where Cowley was. Let alone what kind of goods might be churned out there.

'Saturday.' The Janssen woman, once having downed her coffee, returned the cup to its saucer with a decisive clunk.

Her gaze intent upon Claudia, she did a mental check of her diary which she'd forgotten to bring.

Once sure nothing had been overlooked, she carried on. 'What are you doing this weekend? You're *most* welcome to come to me if you happen to be free. My two are sports mad and spend every bit of their leisure time at some event or other. Come rain or come shine. And my Karl will be off to the races.'

As she spoke, she pushed the dirty crockery to one end of the table. The waitress collected everything with a smile as Bel continued. 'It's Royal Ascot this week as no-one needs telling and the reason this place is heaving.'

Confronted with another snippet of local info Claudia gave an all-knowing nod. Though in truth, was ignorant of anything to do with the horse racing calendar, and despite the display of flags, banners, and other paraphernalia on every street corner, she didn't have a clue. The church diary was the only thing concerning dates Claudia could get her head around. And today, her mind was on other things.

'Not that my Karl's a gambler' Bel continued the equine type of banter. 'And they bring the best in Europe over for Ascot.' She went on.

By which time, into her date's every expression was written the message - just like those Royal Ascot horses, Claudia Elliott was raring to go. Her very next remark brought confirmation.

'*Saturday.* Do we have to wait until then?'

Bel stuck to her guns.

'Oh, come along. It's Wednesday already. And we don't want to rush things. Now do we?' As the Janssen woman whipped off her specs, Claudia found herself gazing into a pair of hazel, almond shaped eyes. Before, leaning in over the table, chin cupped in hand, she was treated to several flutters of the longest pair of lashes one could imagine.

'Let's savor each moment on our journey of discovery.' Bel Janssen crooned. 'Much more exciting. Don't you think?'

Claudia had never been secretly more thankful to have her device in place, not wanting to miss a single syllable of what the worldly-wise Annabelle Janssen had to say. S

And, upon realizing there was no point arguing with this woman, Claudia gave her assent.


So, it was to be on a blistering hot, if rather breezy Saturday in mid-June Claudia waved goodbye to her virginity. And what better place could there have been to host the occasion than Bel Janssen's ultra-modern home. Just as the first race of the day got underway a few rising trots down the road.

With passion mounting in perfect time to those jockeys getting into their saddles, Claudia had good reason to believe she, for one, had backed a winner. Vivienne Barclay's charms were extinguished from mind, soul, and body as she gave herself to her first female lover.

Bel had helped Claudia out of her thin cotton top and white lace bra. As soon as their first lingering kiss came to an end and while seated on one of two matching leather sofas. Bel had then undressed to the waist, before enfolding Claudia again in her arms. Claudia gave a sharp intake of breath as the women's bare flesh made contact. Bel softly

moaned as her firm rounded breasts grazed
Claudia's ample bosom. Her lips sought her lover's
again and again, triggering in both women *the* most
indescribable sensations. Once able to tear herself
away, Bel stood up to step out of a pair of white
culottes, to reveal a pair of shapely and deeply
tanned legs. Taking Claudia by the hand the two
women trod barefoot the thick carpeted staircase.

'In here' Bel whispered with what breath she
could muster, letting go Claudia's hand to usher her
into the master bedroom. Claudia was on fire with
desire and trembling like a leaf while, still on her
feet, her normally adept fingers fumbled to undo the
two hooks on her skirt. When she finally managed,
the skirt fell to the floor. Time then stood still, as
the women's journey of discovery began. Until
some two hours later, they lay, replete. Bodies still
entwined, on top of the cool cotton bedspread.

And it would get even better, Claudia told herself.
As she basked in her new sense of awe and of
wonder. At that first glorious release from her
torment and unfulfilled longings.

# CHAPTER 8

28th NOVEMBER 1985
PARKLANDS   KENTLEY MANOR

My dear Claudia….

This has not been an easy letter to write. I have
thought long and hard how to break things to you…

A ripping sound and the sight of fragments of
paper floating to the ground brought Claudia's mind
back into focus. Rage. Anguish. Unbearable pain.
These and other emotions had caused her to flip as
she read then re-read Bel's letter. Its contents
disguised by the prettiest of stationery…
'relationship not been going well for some time.
Wonderful memories have, however, been made.'

A high-pitched shriek had reverberated around
the Elliott's kitchen and beyond. The postman
making his way back up the close overheard it as he
drew level with Parklands. He was accustomed to
hearing and seeing all sorts on his rounds though,
and it was his policy never to interfere.

Claudia had been standing, gazing gloomily at
the drops of rain beginning to fall on the sitting
room windowpane when she had espied Mr Postie
turning into their drive. She'd gone to the hall and
gathered the single item from the mat. Upon
recognizing the writing, she had ripped open the
envelope. Then within minutes its contents had
turned to shreds. Staggering into the dining room,
she had collapsed onto a chair. Her rage giving way

to a deep sense of rejection and despair. With racking sobs, she had buried her face in her hands.

She had known it was coming, of course. One cannot be immersed in a relationship with another of the same sex, without reading the signals reasonably well.

'Different game sweetie between two women. We tune in to each other's feelings far more easily than a hetero pair do.' One of many snippets out of the Janssen woman's store of worldly wisdom. Imparted to Claudia on that first date.

Not that she needed telling. Although her and Viv Barclay had not become lovers, they'd shared a deep emotional rapport. Following which it had taken what seemed an eternity for Claudia to come to terms with her loss. And now this.

*Abergavenny.* Claudia reflected, as she bent to pick up the bits of paper. That's where the rot had set in. This was after Claudia had invited Bel along to a Parish Weekend organized by her new church, St Cuthbert's which she'd eventually joined after leaving St Mark's.

'It will be such an opportunity to spend quality time together' Claudia had enthused. While secretly hoping it would prove the means of bringing Bel one step nearer to embracing the Christian faith. Which, despite her wobble, still meant a great deal to her. To such an extent that, once passions were on the wane, their conflicting beliefs had become an issue. Notwithstanding all this, they had experienced some wonderful moments, discovering what pleased each other. In the bedroom and elsewhere. What was more, Claudia had come to love the woman. Despite their differences, Annabelle Janssen had been quite a catch.

Lately though, Claudia had noticed Bel's behavior becoming non-committal, adopting an almost business-like attitude towards her and their relationship. And when they did exchange meaningful dialogue, the same name kept cropping up. Marianne Compton was a fellow lecturer and Claudia had sensed she had a rival. Picking up on Bel's infatuation with another had led her to say

'You're going off me. I can tell.'

'Oh, what sheer nonsense darling. That lively imagination of yours.'

Bel had been quick to deny any change to her feelings. Why had she not said something when confronted? Let her down more gently. Instead of a whole load of feigned excitement, Claudia in her brokenness had thought.

'Oh, I so love Wales,' being Bel's immediate response. But they'd not made love once all weekend. Almost as disappointing was the hopelessness of trying to include her companion in any of the lively group discussions, always a key feature of these gatherings.

'I have seen the light *not to believe*' had been the response, whenever Claudia tried to share the Gospel message. Moreover, Bel had spent most of the weekend aiming to talk anyone willing to listen, out of Christian conviction and into the New Age philosophies she had begun to explore. With her oodles of charm and razor-sharp intellect, the Cambridge graduate could be most persuasive. Given half a chance.

So, in her heart of hearts Claudia had been prepared. Regardless of her overreaction. They had only met twice since that fateful weekend. The final occasion being at the Janssen home with Bel excusing herself to take a call, minutes after Claudia's arrival. A look of horror and disbelief appearing on Bel's face as she replaced the receiver.

'Oh, golly gosh. How did that happen? Am I losing my marbles? I should be in college giving my star pupil her class.' She had remarked, then donned a jacket and driven off.

'Sorry sweetie. Must dash. Be a darling and drop the latch will you, on the way out?' Being her parting shot with Claudia left to make her way home. And that had been that. Until her morning's post had driven the final nail into the coffin.

'Why, oh, why though?' Claudia, again, had cried out in anguish. Bereft and perplexed at the irony of things. Especially since Charles, in his own way, appeared to have come to terms with his plight. And seeing Claudia had, with only slight reservation, let Bel steal her heart.

How cruel, she had lamented. Over a cup of strong coffee. How *unbelievably* cruel. Could life get more painful than this? And how the hell? Yes God. Claudia made no apology to her Maker for swearing. How the hell was she going to get through the forthcoming Festive Season?

With its round of parties and the twelve people to entertain, already invited into the Elliott's midst. For dinner on Christmas Day.

# CHAPTER 9

'I can't love you, Evie. I must be honest. God knows I've tried.'

'Oh, I see. Happy New Year to you too Claudia Elliott. Here I am, two hundred miles from my hometown and family. And you decide you don't love me.' Evelyn May Morris was furious. As well as so dreadfully hurt.

'Evie. Look at me.'

Claudia turned from where she was standing at the kitchen worktop, preparing a fruit compote. Meant as part of her and Evie's New Year celebration meal. Charles had made his way to Brussels to prepare for a meeting next day. The rest of the family were out for several hours, too.

'I'm fond of you.' Claudia paused then went on. 'Deeply fond. I could certainly say that.' It was not enough. Not what Evie needed to hear.

The two women had met in the spring of eighty-six and Claudia had instantly thought she could do with the kind of mothering this demure, well-bred lady, ten years older than her, had to offer. In her favor, Evie was a fellow believer whom Claudia had visited twice on her home ground around the stockbroker belt of Cheshire. From the autumn of that year, they'd enjoyed something akin to a full-blown romance which had filled a gap in both of their lives. Until now.

Evie had been married and given birth to two children. She'd lost contact with one, following her divorce. Clive Morris had brought the petition, citing his wife's 'unreasonable behavior' as the reason for the marital breakdown, after arriving home early from a conference, he had found Evie in the arms of his business partner's wife. Becky Morris had been appalled while son Richard, though remaining supportive, lived up in Cheshire with his wife and Evie's first grandchild, Poppy. Evie had bought a modest property around Kentley. Simply to be near Claudia.

'Oh. You and your fancy talk. Cannot. Will not. Whatever. You're telling me it's over. Aren't you?' I've come all this way and made my home in this characterless God forsaken place, and now I'll have no-one.' Evie started to cry. She got up from where she'd been sipping on a Douwe Egbert's.

As her anger turned to despair, she collapsed into Claudia's arms, sobbing. The celebration meal forgotten. At the prospect of what the New Year appeared to hold. In the life of Claudia Elliott and her latest lover.

The tables, this time though, had been turned. And it was Claudia who had the unenviable task of bringing things to a civilized conclusion. She had no intention of being brutal. It was not in her nature to treat people unkindly. This was especially important as she recalled her feelings of desolation when first Vivienne Barclay, then Anabelle Janssen had delivered their arrows of rejection. One verbal. One written. They had both hurt like hell. So, she'd a good idea how Evie would be feeling.

Evie rested her head on Claudia's bosom. Claudia ran a hand over the fluffy bouffant hairstyle, taking in the fragrant blend of the John Freida hairspray and Tresor perfume.

'I know. It's hard' she crooned. Taking Evie by the shoulders, she drew back to look deep into her bluey grey eyes. Filled now with anguish. She placed a hand either side of Evie's waist. 'I hadn't planned this I swear. I was looking forward to a nice lunch before our first new year snuggle wuggle between the sheets.' She sighed and released her hold.

'It was when you suggested the holiday in the Swiss Alps. Honestly, I cannot. You know how I hate flying. I'm a bag of nerves each time I go to Provence.' Claudia was searching for the right words. Words of reassurance and of consolation. She took a deep breath and looked straight at Evie.

'Let's be brave, as well as thankful for what we *have* shared. Then try to let go. You must try my love. We both must.'

Evie sought the comfort of Claudia's bosom once again before lifting her head to search her face.

'OK. Forget the holiday.' She knew she was clutching at straws but was resolute in her bid to rescue not just the day but the entire situation. 'We don't have to *fly* anywhere' she pleaded. 'What about the Rhine cruise we promised ourselves? Or, if you don't fancy that, a coach holiday would be nice. Why don't we go have a look at the Dutch bulb fields? Belgium, too, is supposed to be pretty.' Evie went on. 'See what you can glean from Charles.'

Charles Elliott had never been one for holidays. He reveled in the idea of his wife going off on these trips with her friends, lovers, or whatever role these womenfolk happened to occupy in her life. Whoever Claudia had around her when her thoughts turned to taking a vacation, it suited him fine.

Evie was not through with her pleading.

'Just think how you've loved our jaunts' she continued. 'Oh, *please*, darling. Let's not end things.' She wound her arms round Claudia's neck. At sixty-three years of age, she had no idea how she had come to be at the mercy of such powerful emotions. Emotions capable of reducing her to such childlike behavior. She had yet to discover what Claudia knew. Unrequited love was downright painful, whatever one's age or position in life. And after what had begun as a slow burner, Evie had fallen hard. To find herself painfully and rather naively, perhaps, with hindsight, entangled with another woman.

Evelyn May Grant, as she had been born, was awakened to that which her mother had referred to as a 'dark side' to her daughter's nature when, home from boarding school, she had caught Evie in a clinch with her best friend. It had occurred at the end of a party to celebrate Evie's fourteenth birthday. A sudden attraction had resulted in the girls' goodnight hug turning into a long passionate embrace. Evie's mother had taken her daughter aside, telling her, 'well brought up girls do not behave in such a way.' She had then instructed her to seek out more suitable friends. Friends who did not possess that dark side to their nature.

In her twenties, Evie had married Clive Morris then pushed down any romantic feelings towards her own sex. Until she and Ella Swindley had discovered a mutual attraction at a social event attended with their husbands and which they'd been tempted to explore. Apart from this Evie was every bit lacking in experience as Claudia once had been.

'Take me to bed. Oh, go on. One last time.' Evie pleaded, thinking if they got themselves undressed and into Claudia's warm and welcoming bed, the relationship would set itself to rights. She clung to her as they stood to one side of the kitchen window.

'Forget lunch. Forget holidays. Forget everything. Except *this*.' She pressed her bosom hard against Claudia's. 'Let's be true to what we know ourselves to be. Oh, do come on.'

Claudia was unresponsive. Where once any touch from Evie would have evoked intense pleasure, today there was nothing. The Christmas break had confirmed what she had suspected, all along. Despite her aching need, she was not in love with this lady. And though the relationship had brought a measure of healing, the attraction ignited through that need had died for Claudia. The rampant desire she had experienced for Viv Barclay would always be a world away, she realized, from anything she felt towards Evie, as she pushed her gently aside.

'No. Please Evelyn. I need to continue with the meal. My three could all be in by teatime. They're bound to be ready to call a halt to the endless round of parties that've occupied every bit of their free time since November. Carolyn might turn up sooner with her new fellow.' Claudia sat back down at the table and went on. 'She's dying to introduce him. A wealthy American who's finally stolen her heart.' She continued before looking away. Although when she next spoke her tone had softened.

'The chemistry's not there anymore. You could call it bad timing. Or seen in a different light, perfect timing.' Lowering her head, she ran a hand over her denim skirt in a smoothing gesture. Before looking Evie's way once again.

'Well. You know. New Year. Fresh start. Resolutions and all that.'

Evie sat opposite her, motionless, with Claudia resolving to stay positive.

'Look. Why not stay for lunch? I can rustle up a light bite for we two. Instead of that calorie ridden spread I was planning. I, for one, need to lose...' she hesitated. 'Well, heaven knows what I've put on over Christmas. Let's not ruin the day' she remarked a little too brightly, then gave a sigh followed by 'Oh dear.' Getting up, she went to stand at the kitchen window. She twisted the cord to open the blind and gaze out over the lawn still blanketed by the morning's deep frost.

'Despite what I said, forgive me. It's not the best start to the year. Is it?'

Evie buried her head in her hands and gave a sigh of resignation. But when she spoke, retained her composure. Having taken onboard Claudia's comments, she had made one New Year's resolution.

'Thanks for the offer. But don't worry about lunch. I'll be off. There's Lucy who was widowed in the autumn. You know, the friend I do my stints with at the library.' Evie had taken on voluntary work at Kentley library. And it could prove her rescue package, she reflected now. In the light of events.

'You're right' she went on. 'Let's look back on what we *have* shared and how good it has been. Then we need to move on.' By drawing on her faith Evie was finding the strength to stay dignified. Painfully aware it took two to hold any relationship together.

It would be a long time before she was ready to go forward into anything close to what she had, for two wonderful years, enjoyed here. She must though, seek out new friends and the right ones would prove mutually rewarding, she knew.

'I'll give Lucy a ring the minute I get in and invite her over for a meal' Evie remarked. 'Like me, she's no family around these parts. She'll welcome my call and I've enough food left in my freezer to feed an army.'

She got up just as Claudia walked over to refill the kettle.

'Make it one cup. I'd best be off' she said, heading for the back door. 'Cheerio and thanks' she continued. 'Thanks for everything Claudia. I mean it.' Evie took hold of the gold-plated knob and turned to face her ex one final time. 'And may it be the Happiest New Year you've had in yonks. Not just yourself but the entire Elliott household. I mean that, too.'

Claudia watched Evie disappear down the side of the house and a minute later, get into her gleaming black Ford saloon car, contrasting strikingly, with the morning frost. As Evie drove off, Claudia sat down with her solitary cuppa. And wept.

'Happy New Year Lord' she whispered through her tears. 'How next and with whom next, will you allow this deep need of mine to be met?'

Given Claudia Grace Elliott's tendency to toward manipulaton, her God in His Supreme Wisdom was not quite ready to reveal to His daughter, what was around the next corner.

Part 2

# CHAPTER 10

SUMMER 1980
STANBOROUGH  NORTHERN ENGLAND

The hall clock chimed eight as D I Foster pulled up
a chair in the Foster couple's kitchen diner. He
eased his burly, six-foot two frame on to it.
    Thanks for waiting. I thought yer'd have had
yours. Traffic was terrible getting out er Leybridge.'
'Leybridge?'
    The D I picked up his knife and fork, sat back and
surveyed the offering.
    'Looks good. Holy Toad.'
Jackie glared at him across the table.
    'What sort of thanksgiving prayer's that?'
    'Nay, lass. No prayer. Just a bit er fun. Toad in the
hole to christen it right.  Hey! But while we're at it,
best thank the Good Lord for His bountiful
provision. And for t'prettiest wife in t'whole county
for putting it all on mi plate.'
    Jackie closed her eyes tight. She threw her apron
up over her face and wiped her weary brow. Did she
have to be subject to this? Since little Laura Jane
had arrived on the scene, Ivan had regressed to his
own childhood. The minute he was off duty at the
station. Having a three-month-old rival for his
wife's attention, twenty-four seven, had been quite
an adjustment. After five years of their cozy
twosome.
    The conversation wasn't likely to get better,
Jackie knew. And it didn't.
    'Aven't yer had t'news on?'

70

She was struggling to digest her first mouthful of dinner.

'No. I'd just got Laura off when it was starting. Her hearing's as sharp as mine and I didn't want to risk waking her.' After spearing a segment of sausage with her fork she glanced the inspector's way, fork and food held in midair. 'It's been one of those days. I'm all in. I'd just managed...'

'T'loony Liverpudlian's been at it again.' Her husband cut in. 'Got called over to t'East Lancs HQ. Been there all day, liaising wi 'em. Reet bloodbath.'

Jackie was aghast when, carving his way through the battered bangers his gaze never flinched from the food. 'I tell yer, if yer could've had a butchers at t'scene er crime shots. Aye. *Butchers.*' He banged the blunt end of his fork on the glass topped table. Impressed at his own turn of phrase. 'That sums it up I reckon. Can't think of a better express...'

'Ivan. Please.' Jackie dropped her cutlery with a clatter. Horror and disbelief reflected on her tired features.

'Sorry.' He grunted.

'I should think so.'

The inspector still didn't lift so much as an eyebrow; he was that engrossed in his meal. Jackie got up. For all his redeeming qualities, and there were a few, Ivan's mentality combined with his gross insensitivity was more than she could handle on days like today. If she was honest, she had always harbored the notion her husband's taste for the lurid had played a part in his choice of career. That said, fatherhood and their newly discovered Christian faith had softened him a tad. His workload had got to him today, that was all. And no wonder.

She shunted the remains of her meal into the bin and replaced Ivan's empty plate with a dish of rice pud. Then, as grim details of what her husband had brought home began to sink in, she changed the subject. As he topped the pudding with a great dollop of jam, Jackie reminded Ivan of the Bible study due to take place the following evening at their church, St Swithun's.

'I've asked Gemma to sit. I expect we'll start with some prayer. Vince and Amanda are leading, and they sure know how to pray. It's terrible. All these murders. God knows where it'll end.'

Vince and Amanda Samuels were an Anglican vicar and his wife. They'd been sent from the south to assist with the goings on at St Swithun's. The charismatic movement begun in the seventies was well underway. By the eighties, enough books had been written on the subject to fill a library. And those needing reassurance they had not lost the plot or been brainwashed when they found themselves speaking in an unknown tongue, only had to turn in their Bible to the New Testament Book of Acts.

'Aye well,' Ivan responded. 'Yer not goin` to be seein` me in any holy huddles down there. Officers' briefin`s, more like. Till we catch the bast…the so and so. I've told `em scores er times to widen t'search.' The D I took a huge slurp of the tea his wife had put under his nose. 'There's a lass in t'Midlands would've suffered exactly t'same fate if he hadn't been disturbed.' Ivan tipped the mug up and threw back his head to get the dregs before setting it down with a thud. 'I've begged `em to listen. But will they heck?'

'Will they heck what?' Jackie was at the sink. The clatter of the dishes drowning out most of his ramblings.

'I *said*. Oh, never heed. It's time I switched off
from what I've been dealing wi. Is t'little 'un okey
dokey? It's no good this. No good at all. I hardly get
to see her from one week to t'next.' 'Laura's fine.'
Jackie was beyond complaining. Her troubles
assuming their rightful proportions. Once aware of
events beyond their four walls, she could no longer
justify filling her husband in on how their precious
little monkey had been sick over her cot blankets,
then twice over her. She collected the empty mug in
silence. The inspector heaved himself off the chair.

Jackie took off her apron. 'I'm going up to read.'
She ran her fingers through her out of condition
hair. Probably plastered with baby sick, too, she
reflected, brushing a handful of sticky strands from
her face. 'I'm halfway through that book Mandy
lent me.'

'Oh aye. Which one? Hey. But before yer
enlighten mi, we could do wi a bit more off than
that pinny. Cum 'ere. Yer look ravishin' when yer
all hot and bothered.'

Jackie turned immediately towards the stairs.

'The book's called From Prison to Praise. Now if
you'll excuse me I need to get my hair washed.'

'Well, I'll have a butchers at this 'ere book when
yer done. Hey.' For a second time since walking
through the door, the inspector became impressed
by his own wit. 'I reckon I'd better.... Prison - if
yer get mi drift.. PRISON to Praise. Although it's
them t'other side er t'gates who need ter get their
noses stuck in. I'll see they get chance, an' all on mi
next visit.' He lowered the reading specs he'd
donned to check his morning's post and stared at
her over them. 'That's mi next *official* visit I hasten
to make clear. I've no plans to join t'inmates.'

'Yep. The book's fascinating' Jackie replied, choosing to ignore the rest of the remarks. 'I'll let you have it when I've done. I'll be in the land of nod though by the time you come up' she added, putting a foot on the first rung of the stairs, before lowering her voice. 'I'm exhausted. So don't go thundering about waking us both. Will you?'

She'd had enough of her maternal duties for one day. And more than enough of Ivan's ayes and heys, topped off with the day's grim tidings. All she wanted was a little respite from the daily grind.

These were her thoughts as she washed her hair, before saying a prayer for the early capture of the monster at large. Then, as her head hit the pillow, Jackie was out like a light.

# CHAPTER 11

Her first thought upon waking was Laura must have slept through. It was seven thirty and the baby was just opening her large ebony eyes when Jackie went to check. Ivan had left before first light and if the news he'd come home with was anything to go by, there was no telling when he'd be back. However with their sitter already booked, Jackie began to look forward to seeing Mandy later.

The Samuels wife was not only attractive but was full of a vibrancy seldom found in men of the cloth or their women folk. Moreover, Jackie hoped another prayer session would soon be on the agenda. The two women had taken to driving onto the north Yorkshire moors to commune with God and with nature. They had received some tremendous answers to prayer and were becoming increasingly conscious of the anointing which would fall upon them, the moment they began to intercede for those God placed on their hearts. All typical of the signs and wonders recorded in another book Jackie had read, entitled *My God is Real*.

As time went on Jackie began to feel closer to Mandy than to anyone. Even Ivan. What they were being blessed with felt natural and right. Beyond question, as far as Jackie was concerned. The relationship had become deeply emotional for her, in addition to their spiritual bond. She loved doing the everyday things with Mandy. Even a food shop became exciting if done along with her friend.

One hot July day, the two women shared their usual parting embrace. Only this time, although having brought the prayer session to an end, the anointing remained. Until they were bathed in it from head to foot, as their bodies beneath their thin cotton dresses fused, momentarily, into one.

Jackie had never experienced anything like it. And, back home, she found herself doing some soul searching when Ivan returned from the station.

Despite his faith commitment, on the day in question, the D I had been battling his carnal nature from start of shift to arriving home. He'd failed miserably to turn a blind eye to his colleagues' choice of artwork adorning the back-office calendar. Then, at lunchtime, he'd completely lost it. Upon spotting their cleaning lady enjoying her lunch al fresco. Sylvia Barker had arranged herself and her scanty outfit on a picnic blanket leaving little to the imagination. It had sent Ivan's temperature soaring.

'Hey, that were a reet good dinner. Yer spoiling me. Roast beef mid-week. What've yer been up to I wonder? It must've been hot wi t'oven on.' His hand reached out to pull his wife onto his knee as she went to collect his plate.

'Cum `ere.'

Jackie froze, despite the hot evening air, and she wasted no time stepping out of his reach.

'Don't be silly. I'm sure I've heard Laura.'

'Nay. Yer haven't. She's fast on. I peeped in while yer were up ter yer eyes rattlin` them pots an` pans. Bring yersen `ere. T'little un's fine.'

Jackie still thought she'd better keep her distance. At having found the peculiar longings triggered by the day's encounter with her friend disconcerting. And, though uncertain of their significance, they sure didn't tally with what Ivan had in mind.

It was gone ten by the time she'd got round to clearing the dishes, leaving her wondering whatever had possessed her. Why had she not rustled up something quick on the kind of day it had been, so she could have retired earlier?

Such thoughts were uppermost in her mind as her husband rambled on.

'Christian couple we might be. But I'm still a full-blooded fella yer know.' Inspector Foster was in no mood for excuses and, to Jackie's horror was already undoing his belt. 'I can't remember when I last felt ser randy' he chortled.

Jackie turned immediately to make her way up the narrow Victorian staircase. Once in their bedroom, she undressed, then lay there feeling vulnerable and exposed.

It was so hot though; she'd been desperate to get out of her clothes. But the minute she did, thoughts of Mandy and their time spent outdoors began to invade her mind and to flood her emotions.

Five minutes later, as she was reaching under the pillow for her nightie, Ivan's footsteps came thudding up the stairs. Naked now below the waist, he unbuttoned and whipped off his shirt. Jackie had been hoping, praying even, his ardor would have cooled. It had been a vain hope. And a prayer God had not cared to answer. Finding his wife naked too, was more than he could have dreamed of. It sure was D I Foster's night.

'There yer go, see. Gently does it. No need to rush.'

*Every* need to rush, Jackie mused. Choking back tears. And on that score, despite her husband's note to self, she'd no cause to fret. It was over in minutes.

'Hey, mi lass, that's exactly what the quack ordered. It'll give me a better night's kip than any er them pill popping cronies er mine get.'

He heaved himself off her as he spoke, all thoughts turning to fellow officers he knew to be on medication to help cope with the frequent trauma resulting from life down at the station. 'I hope it were okey dokey for you an'all. It takes two to tango as they say.'

Jackie made no attempt to reply.

What was more Inspector Foster hadn't the foggiest where her imagination had involuntarily transported her to, throughout the entire and unwelcome encounter. She had heard, of course, of women fantasizing about imaginary lovers while making love with their partners. Before coming to faith, at least, she would have said it did no harm. There was more to this than pure fantasy, however. She sensed it. Very deep within. And if nothing occurred to intervene, her friendship with the Anglican minister's wife had every possibility of turning into something much more.

Something with far reaching consequences. For her far from perfect but reasonably secure ten-year marriage.

# CHAPTER 12

## SPRING 1984
## STANBOROUGH

'Mummy, mumee. Where've you been? Daddy said we'd better send out search party when he phoned. Can I have a party on Saturday? You promised.'

'Yes darling. Of course. Mummy went shopping after work. That's all.' Jackie smiled down at Laura while trying to avoid her and the dog, both cavorting at her feet. She heaved two carrier bags onto the kitchen table. Candy the golden cocker spaniel had proved a splendid companion for Laura and the two had become inseparable.

'Sorry to have kept you, Jo.' Jackie yelled to their childminder amid the chaos.

Although hard to believe, their daughter was turning four that weekend. The arrival of Candy had been Jackie's idea. Seeing Ivan's dream of a brother or sister for Laura would not materialize. Not on Jackie's watch, anyhow. Her sense of loss had been great once Vince Samuels announced the previous autumn their time at St Swithun's was at an end. Vince had been invited to take up a parish in East Anglia. It might have been a million miles away for all Jackie cared. She had been on the brink of delightful, if somewhat dangerous discovery when she found herself having to deal with, not only the withdrawal of the Samuels wife's friendship, but the loss of all Mandy and Vince as a couple had come to mean to her and Ivan, too. The Fosters had, nevertheless, continued to attend St Swithun's and the swathes of blessing brought about through the Samuels' ministry continued. Jackie had become involved with the contemporary dance and drama group along with choir membership and other activities. All meaning her feelings of loss had, given time, abated. Especially, once she found herself holding down a job too, when, with Laura in school, she was offered a part-time post in Patients' Welfare at Stanborough General. A similar position to one she'd held before having Laura, and therefore, suited her. And when a vacancy occurred for an office supervisor she was offered that, as well.

It is within this very context, however, Jackie is confronted again, by that which had captivated her so powerfully, yet so briefly, in her friendship with the Samuels wife.

Sonia Bellinger was the latest recruit to join her team. Jackie had been one of the selection panel who had favored her for the position. Sonia possessed an impeccable CV with a sense of style and good looks which only added to her credentials. And soon it was to be her first morning.

'Jackie, this is Sonia.' Malcolm began, adding 'I know you two have met. But would you mind taking her round to meet the others?'

Jackie got to her feet and gave Sonia her warmest smile as Malcolm headed back to his desk.

'Hi. Welcome to the mad house.' Jackie held out a hand of greeting before going on 'I expect Malcolm's shown you your desk.'

'Nope. Been shown nothing.' Sonia's eyes had held Jackie's for several seconds before Jackie spoke again.

'Oh well. Follow me.'

What fantastic eyes. So beautifully dark and expressive being the first impression the new woman was to make upon Jackie. And as she led her to her desk, recalled the same impression those eyes had made on her at the interview when asked whether she had family commitments.

'Nope' had come the swift reply, as the two had held each other's gaze then. And so today, once introductions were out of the way, Sonia was quick to settle in. As the two women found themselves hunched over the same desk staring at a screen for hours on end, two things became apparent. Firstly, the age of technology had arrived and secondly, the new gal on the block was not going to disappoint.

As trust between them grew, it was during a coffee break Sonia confided she did belong to the faith but had not attended church in ages. This had led Jackie to suggest she might try St Swithun's. Seeing she lived not a stone's throw from its doors and led, surprisingly, it emerged, something of a solitary life.

'Nope, I'm fine' had become her reply to this and every other non-work-related issue. Leading Jackie to the conclusion it would be wise to let their relationship develop at a purely professional level.

Wow, though. Despite, or even *because* of this, Jackie could not fathom what ignited that spark where certain women were concerned. Whatever it was, this latest one had oodles of the kind of chemistry which would make her spine tingle. A certain look or accidental brush of hands would set her heart racing.

Oh bother, Jackie would think. At finding herself having the mother of all tussles with some very powerful emotions. What's the matter with me? I'm the office supervisor. Surely, I'm not...NO. I'm married. So, I *can't* be. What was the word? She wasn't even sure and didn't like labels anyhow. I'm just not made *that* way. These and other similar thoughts whirled round and round in her head. Only to be replaced by, I'm a Christian woman of five years standing and a doting mum, as the battle raged within.

Is this woman feeling it as well? She had asked not only herself but the Good Lord, too. Once convinced Sonia was prolonging the times they spent huddled over the computer. Raising question after question Jackie suspected her colleague knew the answers to, perfectly well without asking.

Three weeks into Sonia's appointment there occurred a leaving party for Malcolm in the large downstairs office. Jackie had never been much of a drinker. But a glass of champers on such an occasion she considered fine. What was more, it soon became clear Sonia was of the mind the odd bottle or two may not go amiss. Jackie was already tipsy as she sipped on her second glass of Dom Perignon while chatting and exchanging jokes with her colleagues. Not too tipsy, however, to count the number of trips Sonia was making to the row of desks pushed together to serve as a drinks bar. And what she absolutely can no longer ignore, is the effect the persistent contact of Sonia's body with her own, is producing. Each time she makes her excursions to the far end of the office and throwing Jackie into turmoil. How is she to handle such a tricky situation, without upsetting the working relationship between herself and her super-efficient right-hand lady?

She recalls a Bible study led by the Samuels, shortly before they moved on. Someone had read out a verse or two in *Romans*, along with a few from *first Corinthians Chapter 5*. To be followed only by silence. Could something contained in those verses have contributed to Mandy's retraction of friendship? Jackie had not been ready to confront it at the time. She was being confronted with it now, though. Whether ready or not. Leaving her excited to the point of elation. Then confused. Terrified even. At the implications of her discovery.

What effect would this 'half blessing-half curse' revelation have upon her marriage and cherished family life? Not to mention her sincerely held beliefs.

It would be several years down the line before Jackie would find meaningful answers. But for now, once having downed two large beakers of super strong coffee, the party was over. As, stepping into her pristine white Opel Manta, off she drove. Out of a town beginning to heave with teatime traffic. And with something far more pressing on her mind than what she could do for their tea.

Furthermore, a day intended to be the one, on which she bid fond farewells to a colleague, had turned into one Jackie would never forget. For totally separate and quite other reasons.

It would now be a day etched upon her mind forever, as the one upon which Jacqueline Rose Foster discovered herself to be - what those living in the twenty first century refer to as GAY.

# CHAPTER 13

'Hey, guess what.'

'I'm too tired for mind games. Spit it out. Or even better, can it wait?' Jackie was just back from dance practice with Moving Lights when the realization hit her she was not as sprightly as she'd once been. She was kicking off her shoes when Ivan launched in.

'I've got mi promotion.'

'You have?'

'Aye. An' not a bloody minute before time.'

'Sounds good. Except for your choice of language. But give me a mo. Or there'll be a puddle.' Jackie crossed the hall to the cloakroom, then soon as she'd settled Candy down after her whoops of greeting, headed for the kitchen with Ivan swiftly behind.

She felt a dig in her ribs.

'So, how do yer fancy yersen married to Detective *Chief* Inspector Foster? An' how would yer like to go live on the sunny south coast?'

'What? Where?' Jackie was caught off guard. It was true her husband had played a key role in getting one of the UK's worst mass murderers convicted at the end of a three-year search. But that was way back.

'Seaport's where we'll be bound.' Ivan continued with a flourish. 'Seaport in Hampshire. Been there once as a kid. Any road, big rise in salary, it'll be. So, yer needn't worry Lady Foster. Yer'll not be needing to grace `em wi yer presence down at t'job centre.' Another prod of the ribs swiftly followed.

'Hey. An` yer never know. Change er scene might do t'trick.'

'Ow. Will you stop *that*?'

Jackie gave a huge yawn.

'What are you on about?'

'Need yer ask? Having stepped back, he moved in on her again thrusting an arm so tight round her waist, she thought she'd pass out.

'Change er scene. Wouldn't surprise me if it turned out t'answer to mi prayers. For that little brother or sister once you an....'

'Whoa, slow down,' Jackie cut in. She'd only gone from cloakroom to kitchen and Ivan had the three of them turned into four. Living in a place she'd hardly heard of.

He decided to keep his hands to himself but persisted in standing over her as she cradled the mug, making the swirly froth on top of the drink the focus of her attention, while praying he'd go sit down. But he was soon off again.

'It'll be great. All er them new seaside spots waitin` to be explored.'

'Excuse me.' She elbowed him out of the way and went to sit at the far end of the kitchen. The heat of the night combined with the unfamiliar smell of alcohol on his breath was making her nauseous. She pushed the cocoa aside.

'Look I'm whacked. I'm thrilled for you...well, for *us*. But it's too late to discuss it right now. All that prancing about after a day's work. Did you pay Gemma what we owed her for sitting?' Diversion tactics were called for, till she could approach things with a clear mind. She could hardly be over the moon at the prospect of such upheaval before she'd finished her nightcap.

Sure, her work situation hadn't improved as time sped by. But she was unable to visualize saying goodbye to their present lifestyle. Along with the job and all she held dear. And what about Laura? How would the change affect a six-year-old nicely settled in school?

Jacqueline Rose Pemberton had been brought up around north Yorkshire. The east coast with its cold sneaky winds had been good enough for her parents when they'd wanted a trip to the seaside. She had been an only child and, first her mother then her father had died relatively young. Her mother from cancer and her father from a broken heart which had ushered in a severe stroke. Meaning she had few family ties. Just an aunt and two cousins who she rarely saw.

Ivan wasn't ready to let the matter drop. The usual plonk down of whatever he happened to have in his hand in moments of inspiration soon followed. On that occasion it was a beer bottle landing with force on the worktop. Undaunted by his wife's lack of enthusiasm, he'd cracked open a second bottle from the pack of pale ale he'd picked up on his way in.

'Well, let's pray about it' he persisted. 'Then we'll have a butchers at t'map. T'chief super's taken it for granted I'll accept. An' I've told him I'll confirm when we've talked it over. Me an' thee, that is.'

'We will.' Jackie reassured him. 'But..'

'But what? 'Ivan took a swig of the ale.

'But not now.' She slid off the stool she'd parked herself on and went over to give her husband a peck on the cheek. 'Goodnight and God Bless. And Congratulations of course' she added before turning away.

Ivan's response was to down the rest of his ale and crack open another, while letting a side of the fridge/freezer unit take his seventeen stone weight. He glowered at Jackie making her exit.

DI Foster had the stamina of an ox and could function on far less kip than his wife. So, he was welcome to crack open another bottle then another, and to stay up till daybreak. Jackie was in no mood yet for celebrations.

As she goes through her nightly routine, she recalls an old work colleague's experience. Roy Bennett had, in desperation, re-applied for a job at the hospital after moving his family to Sussex. At the end of six months, they had been desperate to move back. Disillusioned by the entire venture. Even their kids couldn't settle. Roy had said.

Still though, the Bennett's weren't Christians. Not as far as Jackie knew. Surely their own situation was a different kettle of fish. Once they got down to some more serious prayer and discussion than she was able to entertain right then. And, after which, if they both experienced a sense of God's peace, they would act. It could be her

Heavenly Father's way, Jackie reasoned, as she undressed, of resolving the conflict in her workplace.

She had long since moved the desks around on some false pretext, but really to put distance between her and the problem. Still though, whenever Sonia Bellinger walked into the room, Jackie's eyes would light up and her whole being would come alive. No matter how many prayers she sent up, her heart would skip a beat whenever Sonia walked in the room.

Seaport, wherever it was, and Jackie couldn't be sure without consulting their map, would be a world away from what she faced here. She would miss lots of people for certain. However, when God closes a door He opens a window, was a phrase she'd heard bandied around church. Jackie began to wonder until sleep overtook her, exactly how wide such a window of opportunity might be.

Was the Foster family on the brink of a new and exciting adventure? There were, at that moment, more questions than answers. But bags of time ahead to find out.

# CHAPTER 14

'It's streets warmer down there, I tell yer.'

Four months had passed since Ivan's promotion. A typically changeable British summer had turned into a pleasantly warm golden autumn, in the leafy North Yorkshire countryside. The Foster home was in the hands of an Estate Agent with still no buyer. Ivan had been living in Hampshire three months, travelling back to be with the family whenever he could. That weekend, he was on such a visit.

'A bloke from Pontefract's just joined t'ranks wi t'wife and two bairns set to follow.'

As Ivan continued Jackie was transferring from their newspaper wrapping, three chunks of flaky white cod hidden in crispy golden batter and accompanied by a mountain of chips. The inspector had been unable to resist a visit to his local chippy.

'I pity those southerners trying to understand the guy. If he's even broader than you.' Jackie remarked. Ivan having been brought up and started his policing around Wakefield before his transfer to the North Yorkshire force.

'Aye, well, at least wi can translate for each other.' Ivan replied, as Laura began to throw chips at Candy who was sat prettily on her haunches.

'Laura. How many times have I told you not to feed her at the table? And you,' she yelled at Candy. 'Basket.'

Jackie was finding their current lifestyle a challenge. Since starting school, their daughter had taken her cheek to a new level.

'I'm not hungry. I've eaten the whole packet of sweets daddy brought me. All except the green ones. I gave them to Candy` cos they look like the horrid veggies the dinner lady makes us eat. She can have all my chips and a big bit of my fish. I feel sick.'

Laura made a retching noise as Jackie shot Ivan a look of exasperation. She wouldn't have been surprised if dog and child were both about to throw up. She had risen early, let Candy into the garden then grabbed some toast before Laura woke. She'd been rummaging for something to wear when Ivan had seized his opportunity.

'Hey. Yer more irresistible than ever after a fortnight not seeing that gorgeous body er yours. I don't half miss them cuddles we used to 'ave at t'weekend. I could think er nowt else drivin' up. It's a wonder I didn't prang..'

Laura, mercifully, had burst in and leapt onto the bed to give her daddy an enormous hug. Her and Jackie having been in the land of nod when he'd arrived late Friday. Laura bounced around now between her parents as Ivan reached down the side of the bed for his bag.

''Ere we are princess.' He'd undone the front flap then flung the bag onto the floor. 'Have a look in there.'

The girl had jumped down and dived in.

'Ooh, yummy. Jellybeans.' She'd danced from the room, rustling the bag of sweets, calling to

Candy. While Jackie leapt out of bed, grabbed her dressing gown to immediately follow.

And now several hours later, here they were, washing down the nation's favorite take away with a gallon of Yorkshire tea. When two friends of Laura's turned up to play, the time had arrived for her parents to have a heart to heart concerning their house sale.

An offer of employment at the local Law Courts commencing January was the thing which had finally convinced Jackie the move was on. Then affirmed, following an exploration of the area straight after her interview. Her anxiety at uprooting Laura resurfaced, however, at hearing the squeals of laughter coming from the garden.

'A couple put in an offer as I said on the phone. Then their buyer pulled out,' Jackie began.'

'Aye. Pity.' Ivan grunted.

'Yep. There's been three more viewings since we last spoke. But not a peep back.'

She took a deep breath.

'Nothing's going smoothly, so it looks like being a long process.'

She paused then went on. 'It's hard to be sure.'

'*Sure*. What aren't yer sure of?' Ivan bellowed.

'Well, you know.' She concentrated her attention on stacking the plates and putting Laura's leftovers aside to possibly reheat. To distract from his anger.

'Well, whether we're doing the right thing' she continued, when finally looking his way, the color of the DI's face was visible evidence of a sudden rush of blood to his head.

'I think we should pray for a sale soon. If we're all meant to go,' she carried on regardless. 'I'm going to miss all the folk we've come to know at church,' she continued. 'And I'm worried about Laura. She's told me three times she doesn't want to leave Stanborough Infants' and her friends.'

Jackie, too, was going to miss Sonia. Although there was no way she was willing to admit that.

'*Don't* change yer mind now. For the love of God.' Ivan roared. 'Course we're all meant to go.' He got up to collect the dinner plates and just about threw them into the sink. Caring not a jot one sustained a deep crack. He strode from the kitchen diner toward the back door.

'Anyhow, I've summat that's bound to change yer mind.' Returning from his vehicle he dropped three glossy brochures onto the coffee table, Jackie having gone to sit in the lounge.

'Have a butchers at these if yer please, at yer leisure.' Ivan had announced as the top brochure slid from the pile, landing on her foot.

'Ouch' she'd cried. With, minutes later, the cries turning into those of delight.

'Wow, these look fab.' Jackie held up a page featuring a development close to the center of town.

Ivan having taken up a position in the armchair opposite her on the sofa. Hands clasped, resting between his knees, he tried to read his wife's face.

'Which ones?' He enquired forthwith.

'These.' She exclaimed. 'Four bed detached. Large garden. Conservatory. Double garage. The lot.'

Ivan's blood pressure returned to somewhere near normal.

'Aye, well. If they're what tickles yer fancy there's some lively churches near an' all. I poked mi head into one last weekend.' He scratched his forehead. 'T'Lantern, I reckon it's called.' He went to sit next to her and put an arm around her shoulder.

'There's t'last two er that spec just going up. Should be ready bi Christmas. Do yer fancy drivin` down wi Laura for a butchers on mi next weekend off?'

'Well, provided we can get a buyer here, I do,' she replied. 'Oh my, look at that kitchen.' Jackie couldn't hide her excitement.

Their Victorian semi was nice. Especially with all Ivan had done. Given the time, he was a dab hand at DIY. The idea of a fresh start though in a brand-new house and location was appealing. It could be the very solution to break her free from her stuffy background. And would put an end to the bothersome longings still haunting her in Stanborough. Surely.

'It's not just t'churches.' Ivan had continued to enthuse. 'There're some fantastic beaches near enough for yer to take Laura, an` smashing places for us all to visit on mi days off. Hey' he'd grabbed her hand, squeezing it hard enough to break a bone. She'd pulled the hand free as he gushed.

'An` fancy being able to pop over to t'Isle of Wight for t'day.'

'*I* like Scarborough and the roundabouts. Can we go to Scarborough tomorrow instead of church?'

94

Laura had appeared. Shouting and jumping up and down in front of them. Once her friends went home.

'There's much more sunshine down south darling.' Jackie had coaxed. 'You know how it rained all day on your Sunday school trip this year.' She put an arm out to draw Laura in. With Candy running back and forth at their feet, sensing something was in the air. 'Come look at these lovely posh houses.' Jackie had gone on. 'Then daddy's going to drive us down to the river. We can go on the boats and feed the ducks. Seeing as the sun has managed to visit us today.'

Laura had pushed Jackie away, before running upstairs calling 'I don't like posh houses and I don't want posh friends. Candy and me are staying here then you can't sell my room.' Candy, in hot pursuit, had woofed her agreement.

'Leave her. She'll come round.' Ivan had tried to appease Jackie as they got ready to go out.

By midafternoon the family were enjoying their time around Stanborough with its many attractions, before finishing off in Jackie's favorite tea shop. The only blight on things had been as they came into town from the river. She'd glimpsed Sonia going into Next, then caught sight of another female a step or two behind. Jackie's reaction was to convince herself the two women weren't together. Sonia being the kind of independent character who she felt certain, would go shopping alone. But was not deluded for long after witnessing Sonia slip an arm around the other woman's waist.

All the familiar longings rushed to the surface in Jackie. So that it was only as they were leaving the teashop Laura managed to save the day.

'Excuse me,' she had piped up, tugging at the waitress's apron. 'Can I please have a doggy bag for the rest of my cake?' The little girl had heard the phrase when visiting another restaurant. 'I'm not hungry.' Laura went on now. 'I've eaten too many sweets and we've got a *real* doggy in the car. Please can I have a teeny-weeny bag for her? She's called Candy and she's my best friend.'

The episode had lifted Jackie's mood by the time they left, Laura dancing all way back to the car park with the cake tied in a bag.

On the Sunday they'd had friends round for lunch. And Jackie, having set her sights on a whole new lifestyle was feeling ready, at last, to move on.

'Keep me posted on the Blenheim development,' Jackie had called to her husband later, as he climbed aboard his land rover for the drive back.

'Aye don't worry, I will.' Ivan had shouted, the window of the vehicle still down, as Jackie went on. 'I'm tempted to ask you to secure the corner plot with the bigger garden. I'm wondering if you should put down a deposit before I've seen it,' she added.

Ivan responded with a thumbs up.

'Sounds like a good idea. They're selling right fast,' he'd hollered. Before turning his attention to Laura.

'Bye, mi princess. Don't forget to ring mi soon.'
After which, with two toots loud enough to rouse
the dead, he was gone.

'C'mon little one. It's way past your bedtime.'
The Minnie Mouse clock was telling them it was
eight thirty as Laura clambered into bed in her
Paddington PJ's, clutching Emma Louise, her
newest doll, a present on daddy's last visit.

Jackie's heart swelled with gratitude when, still
on the landing, sorting out her work things for
Monday, she'd overheard the little girl's prayer.

'Please God, get daddy back to Seaport safely.
And please, please let me and Candy find new
friends who won't be too posh when our house gets
sold.'

One to go, Jackie reflected, two hours later as she
tumbled into bed. I hope You have a buyer up your
sleeve soon Lord, being her own final plea that
evening, before dropping off to sleep. A sleep from
which she was only awakened when a woman's
voice announced for the third time, 'It's seven am
and time to get up.'

Another day, another week in her walk with her
Lord beckoned. Jackie wondered groggily but with
growing excitement, what it was destined bring.

# CHAPTER 15

LATE OCTOBER 1986
STANBOROUGH

It was a Monday lunchtime and Jackie was about to pop out of the office when her phone rang.

'Ah, Mrs. Foster. It's Jason at Russell and Hobbs. I'd like to arrange another viewing.'

'Yes course. When would you like?'

'How about Wednesday? Can we say eleven?'

Jackie checked her diary.

'Yes fine.'

'Perfect.' Jason Hobbs replied and put down the phone.

Come Wednesday, Jackie liked the look of the guy in his mid-twenties and the petite blonde at his side. They gave nothing away though. Appearing to leave unimpressed.

So, it was with huge delight she took a call after work the next day. Trevor Jones had put in an offer. She was straight on the phone to Ivan.

'Hi. We've got an offer. First time buyer, as well.'

'What's he offering? It'd best be decent? We can't be givin` it away.'

Ivan was known to drive a hard bargain. Being from a family of large-scale investors. His great grandparents had sailed to Oz on the assisted passage scheme. They'd become highly successful business folk, setting up an iron and steel company. His grandfather Lenny Foster being the only family member to return to the UK.

Jackie took a deep breath.

'Twenty-one, seven fifty.'

There was a silence. Apart from muffled tones in the background.

'Be quiet Fletcher, will yer? I'm speaking to t' missus. And less er t'language.'

Ivan took his hand from over the mouthpiece.

'We'll pray about it. Tell Russell and what nots we'll sleep on it.'

Twelve, Grosvenor Crescent was on the market for twenty-four thousand GBP.

'I thought we could er got a bit more. Have we heard owt from any others that've tramped through leavin' nowt but their mucky footprints behind? Must've been hobnail boots last lot er timewasters had on. Any more tell 'em to leave their clogs or what they have on their feet t'other side er t'door.'

Jackie sighed while waiting for him to shut up. 'There's another couple interested. But they can't sell theirs. Anyway, something's happening, at last.'

'Jolly good. Keep me posted.' He, for once, lowered his voice. 'An' wi any other news. Yer knows what I mean. Pitter patter. Hey. An' I'm not talking raindrops.'

Jackie made no attempt to reply, having blotted out anything which might have taken place in the relevant timeframe to give rise to such hope. His optimism on that score only served as a memory jogger. She was overdue for her review with Family Planning. Every woman's entitled to a secret or two was her philosophy. And this, along with how much of the household budget got blown on new shoes was Jackie's.

Friday afternoon brought another call.

'Hi, Mrs. Foster.'

'Yes. Is that Jason?'

'It is. And I've some news. Mr. Jones has increased his offer.'

Jackie's heart leapt. Having been unable to persuade Ivan to accept the first one. She gripped the phone tighter.

'Oh yes.'

'Yep. Twenty-three, two hundred. He's managed to pull a few strings in the lending department of the building society where he happens to work. His fiancé's dead keen, as well. She adored it.'

'Oh, that's great.' Jackie was chuffed as little mint balls.

'Isn't it just?' Jason Hobbs remarked. 'Get back to me when you've spoken to hubby. Then, soon as he's agreeable, we can get things moving.'

Jackie put down the receiver, made herself a cuppa and picked up the phone again.

'Ivan, it's me. The Jones fellow has increased his offer to twenty-three, two hundred.'

'Aw. Stone the crows.'

'What do you mean?'

'I mean if only it'd been what we're after.'

He had already put down a deposit to secure the house Jackie had fallen in love with, at her suggestion, in the light of her receipt of a job offer, following the interview. Even Laura had caught the excitement. Once Jackie had got her to look at the pictures of the showhouse, she began telling her school friends how she was going to invite them for a holiday.

Jackie's impatience now, as she clutched the phone, took hold.

'Oh, c'mon. Let's not mess about. Just think. We can be in by Christmas. They won't hold my job open. If I can't start on time.'

'I've told yer, we can't be givin`...' There was a sudden pause. Then. 'Okey dokey, let's pray. Over t'phone.'

She'd been doing exactly that in her heart since picking up the receiver. Unable to wait a second longer, she took the lead.

'Lord, we know You are with us in this move. Thank You for settling things in Laura's heart, too. Now, please could You confirm these folk are our buyers? And whether to accept their offer? In Jesus name. Amen.'

'Amen.' Ivan echoed.

There was a moment of absolute silence. Before the chorus rang out.

'Alleluia. We've got our buyer.'


By mid-December, the family were overjoyed to be celebrating Christmas in their new home. In January, Jackie began work at Winwood Crown Court and Laura had started her new school. They were getting to know a few folks at the Lantern. Then, come the Spring, Jackie exchanged her Manta for a snazzy little MX5 sports model and life looked promising. Yet more so once she had weathered Ivan's attempt to re-ignite their love life.

It had occurred on Boxing Day with Laura having been invited to the theatre with two new friends and their parents. *Puss In Boots* was in town.

Jackie had been clearing away the dishes from lunch when, voice raised to that of a soccer fan whose team had scored the winning goal at Wembley, Ivan called down to her from the main bedroom.

'Hey, mi lassie, drop what yer doing an` bring yersen up here.'

Oh, Lord no. Jackie had silently pleaded.

Mortified, upon realizing the window had been left ajar to let in some fresh air, since she'd tidied the room, she dashed up to get him to pipe down.

'Ivan, can you…?'

'Aye, you bet I can' he'd chortled, taking a step in her direction. 'I'm not called Ivan the terrible down at t'station for nowt. An` I'm feeling pretty terrible right now.' The inspector had been filled with glee. 'Just you an` me, mi little Christmas angel, wi time on us hands'

Making a lunge for her, he'd squeezed her so tight she thought she'd pass out. Before there came a flash of inspiration.

'Don't be silly. Laura won't be long. Pantomimes don't go on all day,' she said, removing his hand from over her right breast and pushing him right away.

'Look, you'll have to excuse me. Something from all we've been gorging on has upset me.'
She pulled a face and blurted 'Oh, no. I'm going to be sick.'

Hurrying to the bathroom, she'd emerged several minutes later, wet flannel held to her brow.

'I feel awful,' she groaned. 'I'd best go lie down. I tell you what though' she announced. 'There's a rugby match. Seaport Stunners are at home. I spotted a poster downtown.'

Ivan was no sportsman. But if there was one event he could lose himself in, it was a decent game of rugby.

'It'd be better than any rugby match if me and thee could get us kit off and lie down together. Like t'team we're supposed to be' he'd lamented. Jackie had glanced at her watch.

'Look, time's marching on. So why not get yourself down to that stadium?' With happy wife, happy life beginning to penetrate Ivan's thoughts, as she spoke.

'Aye, I reckon I'd better.' He'd responded.

'I'll be fine if I can rest.' Came Jackie's reply.

'I can't think what could've upset yer' he'd persisted.

'Oh, it'd be that brandy sauce. Far too rich for me,' she had countered.

'Aye, well take it easy while I'm gone. I expect I'll be in good company. Half t'station could be there. Seeing it's been quiet on t'crime front.'

At which he'd donned his overcoat and headed for the door.

'See yer later alligator' he bellowed, adding. 'Oh, an' tell our princess I'll be back teatime if she wants a walk with me an' that hound.'

'I will.' Jackie replied.

Candy, who'd been sleeping off her share of the lunch, stirred and grunted. As with a resounding belch, off Inspector Foster went.

# CHAPTER 16

## SUMMER 1987
## SEAPORT

*Are you a Christian who happens to be gay? Have you experienced rejection in church? If so, we are here for you. Come, be free to express your faith in all-inclusive surroundings. Services every Sunday. Midweek activities too.*

This invitation in a local rag caught Jackie's eye. It was several months into their new life when, despite a glorious summer exploring the south coast, Jackie was feeling low. She was not looking forward to the evening meeting at the Lantern. That tangible presence of the Holy Spirit which had first drawn her there was not so evident. Additionally, those bold enough to bare their souls, sharing day to day personal struggles, ran the risk of marginalization. This had become Jackie's perception, anyhow.

It meant traveling to the other side of town. But that was fine. Providing what she discovered there met her need.

Consequently, when Ivan announced the next evening he needed to put in a full day at the station the coming weekend, Jackie seized her opportunity.

'Oh try to keep Saturday free. We promised Laura a trip to the Moscow State Circus. Remember? We said Chloe and Bethany could come, too.'

'Yes daddy. You did promise.' Laura shouted from the landing.

'Just get back into bed, madam,' Jackie yelled, taking a break from a huge pile of ironing. 'It's turned nine o'clock and the conversation wasn't for your ears.'

'Well, I didn't mean to listen. I got up for a wee and heard daddy's big voice.'

'You'll hear it in a minute, mi lady.' Ivan bellowed. 'If yer don't get back into bed. And there'll be no circus or owt else. Do as yer told. Then we'll see.' He was standing, leaning his heavy frame against the wall. The iron gliding back and forth across his shirt, lulling him into a hypnotic like state, working in Jackie's favor, as he spoke.

'Aye.' He replied without hesitation. 'T'circus'll be light relief from what t'bobbies on t'beat are dealing wi down there. Eighty-nine-year-old some so and so's beat up and robbed. All for a few bob an' a packet er fags. T'poor bug...t'poor blighter's still in IT. They're waitin' for him to come round to get some sort er statement.'

'How dreadful. I reckon the circus should do you, as well as Laura, a power of good.' Jackie replied.

'Aye. It'll be a miracle if he recovers. Put him on t'prayer list. Will yer?'

She'd gotten her lead.

'Yep. Sure will. Although, this Sunday I'm thinking of doing something different.' She paused for breath.

'I've asked Laura's pal's parents to pick her up for Sunday school in case you did happen to be working. Then I'm heading for 'Castlehampton?'

'Castlehampton. Yer not thinking er shopping on a Sunday. Surely.'

'No. I'm going to try a new church. I think we're getting a bit,' she hesitated then went on. 'Well, a bit stale. I'm not growing in my faith there.'

'Oh. Can't think why.' Ivan was dubious. 'We have some right good services. It's what you put in, you've got to remember, lassie. That's what counts. As much as what yer get out er such things.'

'I know. But I'm going to give this new place a try.' Jackie set the iron on its stand and put a hand to her back.

'Well, so long as yer home to give Laura her grub. Can't see what t' idea is. Going all that way for a service. But there's no point mi trying to lay t'law down in this household.' Ivan went on. 'All that scriptural mullarky... husbands should love their wives an` wives should obey their husbands. Oh, where the heck is it?' A flash of inspiration followed. '*Ephesians*, I reckon. Aye, that's it. *Ephesians 5*.' He was recalling a passage he'd often flicked through and tried to make sense of.

'Nope, there's no point at all.' Jackie stood the iron back on its stand while Ivan decided to make himself useful putting the newly ironed shirts on hangers. Returning to the task in hand, Jackie took the opportunity to drive home the point.

'You'd best keep your I'm in charge badge for the station. Anyway, Des and Elaine have said they're happy to have Laura till I get back.'

Jackie had staunch reservations when confronted with an overly strict application of some especially difficult and stern passages of Scripture. She'd prayed about that aspect of her faith a great deal. Before reaching the conclusion a degree of flexibility was needed, concerning some of the more contentious passages. Particularly those alluding to the gay issue. For believers who were single, at least, there surely had to be scope for a few lashings of good, old fashioned common sense. When one heard, as one did, of gay people having taken their own lives. Jackie had witnessed, firsthand, the anguish suffered by the family of a seventeen-year-old lad from a Christian background who'd done just that. She'd been on duty at the time of the inquest. A prime example of what could happen to a believer who yearned to be open about their sexuality. Yet knowing to do so was going to result in conflict. At finding themselves, not only at odds with their leaders, but often fellow worshippers, too. Then excluded from personal leadership. Regardless of any sense of inner calling. Or sometimes offered so-called deliverance ministry and a change of lifestyle, to put them in the running for inclusion.

So, what did those Biblical passages relating to same sex relationships really mean? Jackie had taken time to ponder. Bearing in mind, when all's said and done and, according to *Romans 3 verse 23* '(for) all have sinned and fall short of the glory of God.' Why was it the gay people, out of all listed in that passage, were the ones most singled out to repent? When confronted by such dogma Jackie would think of Sonia Bellinger and the way she'd finally confided to Jackie how she was driven from church. For exactly those reasons. Well Jackie, in all sincerity of heart, was not going to succumb to that sort of pressure. Without working things out for herself. Her main authority in support of such a conviction being a passage in *Galatians*. *Galatians 3 verse 28* makes plain there is *no* discrimination based on gender; along with various other criteria.`There is neither Jew nor Greek, slave nor free, male nor female, for you are all one in Christ Jesus.` Again, as translated in the NIV.

What else could all that mean? And whatever interpretation an individual believer, belonging to any branch or denomination of the Christian church might reach, surely *love is love.*

Lust, of course, pure lust being a different thing. However, if two people loved each other, in a romantic or any given sense of the word, especially for those unattached, it did not matter a jot whether they were of the same or, of the opposite sex.

Seeing there was so little genuine and sincere love of any kind in the world, left Jackie unable to understand why the church should make such a fuss. What was more, if her own marriage should happen to come under scrutiny, it was up to her and Ivan how they handled Jackie's discovery. And she was jolly glad Ivan took the same view. With the result that, once lesser issues, personal to their individual lives, were sorted between them, the couple began to jog along nicely.

Especially with Jackie's need well on its way to getting met. Upon her discovery of what turned out a fine bunch of friends. Just as that local ad promised.

# CHAPTER 17

*'We're a family coming home. We have come into our own.'*

This was more like it thought Jackie, a year after stepping through the doors of the Community Church and, as she sang her heart out in Top Notes, their choir, led by the tremendously talented musicians Gareth and Jamie.

*'It's Your blood that cleanses me. It's Your blood that gives me life.'* As they move into this sacramental song Jackie recalls the warm reception received on her first visit. Waiting at the door to shake her hand had been the tall, well-turned-out man with such kind and expressive blue eyes. Once inside, she could not have failed to be impressed by the enthusiasm of the young vibrant minister, so openly gay. These folks sure had a message to proclaim throughout the Christian church and beyond.

Not that the entire congregation was gay. There were people of every sexual orientation and from all walks of life. Leaving Jackie delighted when Ivan became willing to experience the wonders of what her new church had to offer.

'I've had a right anointing every time I've come wi yer. Summat I'd never have thought possible, after hearing what t'evangelicals churn out. Hey,' he'd even boasted, 'there's not many a congregation can claim to have a significant police presence among 'em for Sunday worship, either. Could be right handy. Should a rumpus break out.'

At this Jackie had simply grinned.

Their discussion was taking place over lunch on the terrace of a hotel a short drive from the court building. Ivan had professional reasons to visit the Crown court and had invited his wife to join him afterwards. The beautiful sunny day they'd been blessed with, amid the autumn display of color in the hotel gardens, adding meaning to the occasion.

'There's nubdy'll convince me all same sex relationships fall into one lump. Not after what I've witnessed among that lot. An` look at all t'good they do, serving t'community.'

'I know.' Jackie was quick to agree. 'You should have heard Colin though, when I spoke of becoming part of a congregation where the minister was both Spirit-filled and enjoying a gay relationship, too.'

Col Stott was a recent addition to the Lantern. Jackie had shared something of her Community Church experience with him. Hoping he would have been more open to their way of doing things. Being of a younger generation.

'Oh, aye. What'd that upstart have to say?' Ivan was all ears at the mention of the name. Stott had sent a note round changing the date of a Parish Church Council meeting he'd planned to attend for work related reasons, without consulting anyone.

'He launched into an exposition of a passage in *Corinthians,*' Jackie replied. *'First Corinthians: Chapter 5.'*

She took a small mirror from her handbag and began to renew her make up. The lunch of Welsh Hill Lamb Shepherd's Pie followed by Apple Strudel had gone down a treat. Rejuvenated by the fresh air now, too, Jackie recalled details of their discussion.

'He went on about the sexually immoral and the greedy, the swindlers, idolaters, drunkards, and slanderers who claim to be believers. He said we shouldn't even eat or associate with such folk. Once they've been warned. Quoting, he was, from *verse 11* in the NIV. Check it out.'

'Hecky thump.' Ivan remarked. Astonished at his wife's ability to regurgitate all that. And equally amazed at the blinkered response.

'Oh, yes.' He quoted text after text.' Jackie went on. 'For example, *First Romans: Chapter1* and *verse 28* when applied to the previous two verses, says those who indulge in shameful lusts and same sex relations have been given over to depraved minds.'

Ivan was, for once, lost for words. He could only raise his thick bushy eyebrows which just about met in the middle, as his wife carried on. 'In *verses 29* and *30* it refers to such folks having been given over to..' she hesitated, trying to remember absolutely everything she could. 'Envy, murder, and strife. To name but a few. Oh, and deceit, malice, slanderers, God-haters, the arrogant, the boastful, and so forth. You name it. It's there' she went on. Before pausing for breath.

'Ah. But that's t'whole point.' The inspector gathered his blazer from the picnic bench. He needed to be off. They walked towards his range rover, continuing the debate. 'They're not any er that. All er them events. Running themsen` ragged to raise money for folks in need. There's none er t'churches we've been part of bother enough wi any er that. Not apart from t'Sally Army. They do their fair share alright an` act out their faith, instead er just blabbin` from a pulpit. Aunt Edie was a fully-fledged member. She'd be there every Sunday. Rattlin' her tambourine. Till she ate too many er t'cakes she was forever baking for their charity stalls. Then couldn't get into t'uniform. Any road, I remember mi mother used to say they're one er t'few that practice what they preach.'

'Yep. That's quite a point.' Jackie couldn't have agreed more. 'And, as for the Community church crowd, they're anything *but* full of strife and malice. Those gay guys are as gentle as lambs and as peaceful as doves. Some of the most kindhearted, *non*-malicious souls I've ever come across prop that church up. It doesn't make sense.' She looked toward Ivan, her expression transformed into one of radiance at the thought of her new church family. 'I'm glad you're impressed because I plan to carry on to membership. And I was thrilled at being invited to join their smashing choir.'

Ivan no longer discouraged Jackie from spreading her wings. So long as their daughter was not neglected. If Laura's needs were taken care of, which they most surely were, and provided his wife could put some decent grub on the table, which she certainly did, Jackie could please herself where she worshiped. Or whether she partook of formal worship, at all.

`Charity begins at hooam` had been his father, Frank Foster's motto. And, although, with the Holy Spirit at work in his heart, Ivan had cause to question the validity of such well-intentioned but worldly wisdom, it was a good place to start, he still reckoned.

'Yer OK, mi lass.' He would say. 'Just commit all yer doubts an' problems, big and small to prayer. Then let nubdy except The Good Lord Himself guide yer by His Holy Spirit. Let none er that lot at t'Lantern lord it over yer. Telling yer what yer should and shouldn't think. I can't pretend it's easy.' He stopped dead to have a scratch of his head.

Jackie turned to look back.

'Are you OK?'

'Aye. Except for t'bloody mozzies about wi this mild weather,' he chuntered, before catching her up to carry on. 'But I say again an' I'm being right honest; I can see God at work among that bunch. More ner any church I've had owt to do wi.'

It was a gracious confession. One Jackie recognized as her husband's attempt to make sense of their joint walk of faith.

And something she praised and thanked God for. As they hurtled into the last decade of the twentieth century. Ready to take on the world.

**Part 3**

# CHAPTER 18

8<sup>TH</sup> JANUARY 1990
SEAPORT

Jackie was home early. There had been less traffic than usual to clog up her route. She was preparing dinner when the phone rang.

The sales folk are soon back in the saddle was her first thought as she marched from kitchen to hallway. If it was that sort of call, someone was in for an ear full. If not, it would be Ivan ringing to say he'd be late. She could never get the pots cleared away before bedtime and wondered why she tried.

The Foster wife was out of sorts as they trundled into another new year. Despite being established in her job and having made lots of friends at the community church, none of this, nor even a trip to California in the autumn, Laura's first trip abroad, had been sufficient to dispel the onset of a fresh phase of despondency and gloom.

'Seaport, five one four two eight.' She drew breath to put an end to someone's first pitch of the night. Then was stopped in her tracks by a curious kind of warmth travelling down the line.

Words, when they came simply confused things.

'Oh hello. Claudia here. Is that Jackie?'

Who could it be? Not anyone trying to sell her something. Not from the tone of voice and calling her by her first name.

'Yes. Jackie here. Who am I speaking to? Claudia, did you say?'

'You sound faint, there must be something wrong with your phone' was the caller's next remark.

Jackie took the receiver from her ear and stared into it. Who on earth was it? And what was the matter with their phone? She tried again. Louder.

'Claudia?'

'Ah, that's better. I'm Claudia Elliott' the refined voice continued. 'You wrote to me in November. I've left it until the New Year to get in touch. My Christmas here was pretty hectic. With all the community events I have a habit of getting myself tied up in. As well as the usual round of entertaining.'

Jackie remained mystified as the caller went on. 'So, you're a Christian. And your husband, too. It was jolly good of Angie to put us in touch. Wasn't it? Three cheers for the Three F's, I say.'

Whoa! Now things were clicking into place. Jackie carried the phone into the kitchen with the care one might take when handed a prize trophy in recognition of some remarkable achievement. She pulled out a breakfast bar stool and perched herself on it. The dog got tangled up in the phone cable, following Jackie from kitchen to hall then back again. Feeding time was working its way up the household agenda, Candy knew and was making sure her mistress didn't forget either.

'Go away Candy. Sit. That's right. Sit' Jackie issued the command to the dog before recovering her composure. Thoughts of an early dinner furthest from her mind.

'I'm sorry.' The caller continued. 'Did you say you thought I was Carrie?'

Jackie chuckled. 'Oh, no. I was speaking to Candy. She's our dog.' Jackie slid off the stool and nudged Candy towards the utility room, applying her foot to the animal's hind quarters. She shut the door then settled back on the stool at the far end of the kitchen. She sure liked the sound of this lady.

Though Claudia's Three F's membership was now well established, Jackie's had come about more recently through the *Pink Paper*. This had come to her attention while browsing the Community church bookstall. Her decision to join had come at the end of a traumatic week in which she'd been driven to second guess the sexuality of every female who happened to stray into her orbit.

So desperate was she for an opportunity to express her own sexuality, it had hastened her decision to waste not a minute in sending off her profile to four other members, after plowing through a mountain of details. There had been just one reply from a woman called Angel. Angie Roberts had been quick to make herself plain, however. Like most of her friends at the community church, she was not prepared to get involved with anyone not willing to sacrifice their marriage, before embarking on a gay lifestyle. Having spotted the striking similarities though, she had not minded trying her hand at matchmaker. She had given Jackie Claudia's details and Jackie had shot off a note. The Christmas break was responsible for the delay. All adding to her current despair.

'Well, it's nice of you to phone and yes, I did drop you a note.' Jackie did her best to recollect what the note had divulged before going on. 'Ivan and I were two of many who received the Holy Spirit when a particular ministry team arrived at our church back in Stanborough.'

'Ah. You're from the north then. I did notice the accent.'

Oh, drat. Black mark already. Jackie's heart sank.

'Yes. But we've lived in the south for more years than I care to remember.'

'Well, you haven't lost your accent. Anyway, I'm a believer and belong to St Cuthbert's here.'

'That's nice.' Jackie replied.

'Yes. I'm married to Charles.' Claudia went on, finding herself surprisingly safe to continue. 'He's senior management with the railways. This ache for a woman though, is something which, despite my fair share of material comforts, Chas cannot provide. Bless his heart.'

Jackie sighed.

'Oh. Don't tell me.'

Claudia spoke again.

'I'm amazed to find another practicing Christian in the Three F's. That's a miracle.' Her need to share with someone of the same faith and who understood was leading her to confide in Jackie without hesitation.

'I fell in love with a minister's wife.'

'You did?' Unbelievable, Jackie silently reflected as Claudia continued.

'Yes. It happened where I was worshiping at the time. Couldn't have what I desperately needed from her. Crucified me emotionally and put an end to certain parts of my marriage.'

'Well, I never.' Jackie was wide eyed with wonder. She tried not to lower her voice, despite hearing the front door go and realizing it would be Laura home from her swim class. Jackie was too engrossed in the call, however, to bring it to an abrupt end.

'I found myself attracted to a vicar's wife, too,' she went on. Doing her best not to lower her voice.

'Oh, my. How incredible. We appear to have a great deal in common.' Claudia was more hopeful they were going to hit it off with every word spoken.'

'What does your husband do, by the way? I think you said you work for the courts?'

'Yes. I've studied law. So it suits and gives me my own income.'

'Sounds splendid.' Claudia enthused. Being a staunch admirer of anyone trying to better themselves through education. 'I'm creative and artistic' she went on. 'Together we could be quite an item. What do you think?'

Before Jackie had chance to think or respond to the query about Ivan's job, the conversation moved on.

'Ooh, look, I must dash.' Claudia had seen the clock. 'I've three teenagers and the two still at home will be hunting me down for their dinner.' She gave a funny lighthearted kind of laugh.

'So, what next? Shall I drop you a few lines?'

'Oh, yes please.'

Then we can become acquainted without the accent getting in the way was going through Jackie's mind as she gave her reply..

She had never been conscious of her roots, or the way she spoke. Her down to earth upbringing had taught her not to look down upon anyone. Or let anyone look down on her. It was what Christ taught, too. Wasn't it? That all are equal in God's sight.

'Very well. I'll write you a little letter. Bye for now.'

There was a click at the other end as Laura breezed through, Candy following close at heel, waggy tailed at her release.

'Who was that? Isn't dinner ready? I'm starving.' Laura was munching on a handful of nuts left over from Christmas. 'We're not waiting for dad to get in, are we? Gerry made us do an extra three lengths.'

'Why?' Jackie absently mindedly enquired.

'`Cos he fancies a trip to Barcelona.'

'Barcelona?'

'Yeah. He said with a bit more effort, there's some contenders in our group for the next Olympics.' Laura was, by now, chucking a share of the festive fayre at Candy. With the dog on her haunches, performing her usual trick.

'He's a real joker, that swimming coach of yours. Isn't he?' Jackie remarked. 'Anyhow, dinner won't be long if you make yourself useful by having a go at peeling some spuds. There's a sausage casserole half done in the oven.'

'Who was it on the phone?' Laura persisted.

'Don't you be so inquisitive, madam. Go do as I said and stop feeding Candy *nuts* of all things.' Jackie remonstrated with her daughter. But in the gentlest of fashions. Her mood totally transformed. 'It's time you were learning to carry out a few household tasks, my lady.'

'Why's that then?'

'Because it is.' Jackie responded. A host of reasons crossing her mind while Laura remained unimpressed.

'None of my mates get roped in to do stuff. Anyway, who was it? You still haven't said.'

Laura's curiosity had been truly aroused by the flush of excitement on her mother's cheeks. Along with a fresh sparkle in her wide-awake blue eyes.

Jackie's heart felt incredibly light; she was all at once on cloud nine.

'It was just a lady I know,' she replied, before turning to go check on the dinner. 'Just a very nice lady. Now come along. No more questions. It's time for action. Let's get those spuds peeled between us.'

It was indeed a very, *very* nice lady, Jackie reflected, a half hour later as she dished up dinner, placing a hefty portion aside for Ivan who still hadn't showed up. What was more, if one could fall in love with a person by hearing their voice down a phone wire, Jackie continued to turn over in her mind what was happening deep within her heart.

121

If one *could* fall in love with another by simply hearing their voice, then yours truly was well on her way, to entering a realm which, if she was honest, had always, hitherto, escaped her.

# CHAPTER 19

## 27TH JANUARY 1990
## SEAPORT

'Letter for you mum. It's by the phone. C'mon, we're gonna be late.' Laura picked up her kit bag and opened the door on an icy cold blast. 'Aw, hurry up. It's freezing. You'll have to open your post later.'

Jackie's first task that Saturday morning was to take Laura to her Dance and Creative Movement class in Castlehampton. She grabbed her car keys. Then, heart pounding, hurried to the hall and took the white envelope from the phone shelf. Upon noticing the round, almost childlike handwriting, a wave of excitement washed over her as she slipped the letter in her bag.

Nearly three weeks had gone by since that phone call which had given her heart such a lift. More recently, however, Jackie had allowed the doubts to creep in. With nothing but a stream of bills landing on the mat, it had all, given time to reflect, been part of some kind of dream.

Stepping outside, she shivered and pulled up the collar of her fleece jacket, then dropped the latch and went to open the garage. She got in the car and reversed out. Laura jumped in as Jackie shot her a glance.

'Don't you be so bossy, madam. I'll deal with my post as I see fit. Now, get back out please, pull the garage door down and belt up. Then let's be off, seeing you're eager not to be late.'

With a tut and a sigh Laura flung open the car door and stomped off to do as she'd been asked. Her daughter had, unfortunately, some might say, inherited her father's temperament and Jackie found herself struggling to handle these pre-teen tantrums, on top of her own inner turmoil.

At getting her foot tangled in the seat belt Laura voiced her frustration in language, though barely audible, she knew was unbecoming. Not that it had escaped Jackie's ears. And, normally, Laura would have been checked. But normality, in the Foster household had just been suspended, as off they sped.

Upon leaving home, despite having put the mail in her bag, Jackie had intended leaving it there until she got back. To gloat over with her morning cuppa in her cozy, warm kitchen. But the moment Laura had disappeared into the building where her class was held, the envelope was out and with one clean rip, it flew open. Her hands now all a tremble, Jackie flattened out the two sheets of A4 paper which had been folded into quarters. A tad formal, she found herself thinking. If it hadn't been for a tiny hand painted daffodil on the right-hand corner of each page. And, regardless of presentation, she could not wait another moment to discover what this lady, several years older than her, had to say.

'Dearest Jackie.' Not a bad start. 'Here are the few lines as promised' the letter went on. 'I've been tremendously busy since our phone chat but at last I've gathered some..'

'You can't park here, madam.' A voice that irritating could never be anything but irksome. It

124

was, on that occasion, far more. Her absorption with the mail was such, it took three attempts before the gravelly tones of the warden got her attention. Neither the icy cold air nor the rancid smell of the darkly clad figure's breath streaming into the car had been enough to alert Jackie. Until she realized, at last, she was on the double yellows. Slap bang in the middle of town.

She pressed the lever to close the window, wound down only to remind Laura she was due a lift back with a friend.

'Going,' she mouthed as the window slid up.

*Men.* She fumed as off she drove, the prized sheets of paper on the passenger seat beside her. They floated to the floor as she sped back down the main road, anchoring on, at recalling a new speed camera on that section of carriageway.

Various jobs were lined up to fill her day. Food shopping, the weekly wash and joy of joys, cleaning the oven. The sort of stuff any working mother gets confronted with at the weekend. Unless fortunate enough to have a daily help. She pulled into the drive and gathering up the bits of paper, leapt from the car. Once indoors, she grabbed their laundry bag and with one swoop, bunged the lot into the washer on one setting, thankful Laura had a lift home and for the extra time this allowed.

Twenty minutes later, she was putting the letter back in its envelope. Having devoured the contents three times. First, in the kitchen with her coffee. Then, on the sofa, in their stylishly done out lounge. And once more in her bedroom.

The Fosters had prospered during their time in the south and Jackie was by no means ungrateful. The couple both worked hard for what they'd achieved. This highly prized item she held in her hands though, despite her deep gratitude for the blessings of marriage and family life, this gem of a gift was to bear a significance like no other. In the fullness of time. For Jackie was getting the message this lady was not going to be rushed. But did a little more waiting matter? When on the threshold of something which would provide, that missing piece of the jigsaw.

Already she could memorize the letter's contents. After such a warm introduction had come outpourings straight from the heart. `I so need to hold a woman close. It feels so natural.` Then a few factual details, accompanied by further expressions of Claudia's deepest longings. Signed: `Fond thoughts. C x`.

My first ever love letter from another woman. Jackie became intoxicated with the heady sensation this development gave rise to. She turned the envelope over in her hands then held it close to her heart. Before tucking it away in a compartment of her dresser. Her secret hidey hole she was certain no-one except her knew existed.

Oh yes. Her life was beginning to fill with promise of a happiness she'd hardly dare dream of.

Her marriage, by contrast, from that moment forth became another matter.

For, although she remained confident Ivan would never judge or condemn two same sex people for falling in love and Jackie was sure, very sure, she

126

had, in a romantic sense, done exactly that. With a person she'd not even met.

What would be the outcome? For her. For Ivan. And for Laura? To receive  answers, Jackie was going to need quite extraordinary patience. Every heart leaping step of the way.

# CHAPTER 20

'Oh, you're just like your photo.' Claudia was standing at the station exit, street map in hand when she glanced up to see her date approaching.

Jackie was at once on firmer ground, upon receiving reassurance there were no more unwelcome surprises. Such as the accent had been.

She was spot on, though. Every ounce of patience Jackie could muster was going to be needed, to woo and to win this lady who had captured her heart from the start. And Jackie's patience, never one of her best virtues, had begun to wear thin. But today her outlook was one of excitement and great expectation. After endless phone chats and the exchange of a variety of letters and cards, the big day was finally here.

As Jackie took in the appearance of her date, her heart began pounding in her chest.

Claudia was next to speak again while tucking the map into her bag as they made their way onto the busy streets.

'Did you have a good journey?'

'Yes fine' Jackie replied, falling into step with the older woman. 'How about you?'

Claudia had travelled by train to their agreed venue. It made sense. The rail link was a good one and gave her the opportunity to make use of her free rail pass. Jackie, too, had figured out it would be wise to take the train. Considering the state, she might find herself in for driving.

'Yes. My journey was good' Claudia replied and glancing down to take in more of her date's appearance, gave a smile of approval. Pleased she, too, had taken extra care. Or she could have been the one to be outshone. Jackie Foster was a smart little cookie, Claudia observed, continuing to take the lead.

'Now, I'm not sure what you have in mind. But I know an excellent place the St Giles end of town where we can get a decent lunch without paying the earth.'

It was obvious Claudia knew her way around with little need of a map and Jackie, therefore, agreed as Claudia checked her watch.

'Well, I never. It's past midday.' She turned to Jackie. 'Are you familiar with Oxford?'

'Not really. I've passed through on a couple of occasions' she replied. While in truth, it was her first visit. But she didn't relish the idea of displaying her ignorance concerning the merits of such a fine and historical city. Jackie was all out to impress.

She knew Stanborough, her hometown, like the back of her hand. She could navigate London by tube. Castlehampton and Seaport she had conquered. Oxford, however, was fresh territory to explore. Along with her emerging sexuality.

Notwithstanding all of this, she hoped the place they were heading for would not be much further. Her Italian court shoes were hurting like hell. And they'd only gone a few strides. As for lunch, she didn't think she could manage a morsel, without throwing up.

She was glad she'd gone for the shoes though, as she glanced to her left, keeping in step with this well-turned-out lady. And that's exactly what she was, Jackie was quick to observe. Claudia Elliott was all her polished voice on the phone had hinted she might be. Every inch, a refined English lady. Who she could also now see, to be head and shoulders above her. Despite the choice of a pair of tan leather brogues worn with a blue pin stripe Armani suit and plain lilac shirt. `Tall and well made` had been Claudia's self-description, in one of those early letters and, tall and well-made she certainly was. And outrageously sexy, to boot. In Jackie's eyes, anyhow.

Jackie was, by comparison, of average height and proportionately built. Her best features were her youthful looks and her round, wide awake blue eyes. The neat, cropped head of ash blond hair served to accentuate her elfin features.

As for skills and talents, she had been delighted to learn of Claudia's artistic ability. Thinking it would complement her more academic mind.

They eventually arrived at a sweet looking little bistro. By which time, Jackie couldn't wait to sit down and, after a perusal of the menu, settled for jumbo king prawns with a Thai chilli dip. She adored seafood, so when combined by her total lack of interest in food on the day, the light bite suited her.

Claudia, meanwhile, tucked into a sumptuous
Caesar salad.

At the end of the meal, they paid their bills.
Before off they tottered. With their one glass each
of Chardonnay beginning to take effect, they
meandered alongside what Claudia had informed
Jackie was the Cherwell River, until they came to a
wooden bench. Their stroll, Claudia was also quick
to point out, had landed them at the rear of Oxford's
Botanic gardens. Where Jackie was again, grateful
for the expertise of her tour guide.

'Now how do you fancy a trip up to my part of
the world?' This was to be Claudia's next enquiry.
'I can show you round our famous shopping mall.
Tops for fashion in the whole of the UK' she went
on. Delighted to have, at last, found a woman so
smartly turned out. Jackie having chosen a black
bolero style leather jacket over a crisp white cotton
shirt, while a slate grey pencil slim skirt showed off
her figure.

As the working woman of the two, Jackie had
hoped it might please Claudia to travel down to
Seaport when Ivan was out of town. But had no
intention of turning down any invitation coming her
way.

'Yes, I'm sure I can get up to you' she replied in
a flash. The effect of the wine and Claudia's arm
now placed around her shoulders, leaving her
powerless to resist whatever was to prove the fastest
possible route to get things off the ground. And
though a unique shopping experience did not top
her list of priorities, it would, she'd decided, by the

time Claudia withdrew her arm, make an excellent start.

'Right.' Claudia announced abruptly. As though another world was calling. 'I think we should make tracks. Then we'll be on our way before rush hour.'

It was quarter to three.

'It's been a pleasure I must say. And I'd like to sleep on things now.'

'Fine. I've enjoyed meeting you, too.' Jackie had responded. There being little else she could add.

The pain in her feet had turned into a passion killer no longer to be ignored on that day. Whatever she hoped and prayed lay ahead.

# CHAPTER 21

With no second date on the agenda, it was *the* most romantic *Thank You* card Jackie had ever received which was to pave the way for the next instalment. Jackie responded in kind, before having to endure several weeks which turned into almost two months of silence. But the candle she was holding in her heart for this lady refused to be put out. So, all she could do was to wait and to pray. Until her patience was finally rewarded on the eve of midsummer's day.

'Oh, hello. Sorry it's been so long' the voice Jackie could not fail to recognize announced when she picked up the phone. 'You must have been wondering.' Claudia went on.

'No. Not at all,' Jackie replied in her most matter-of-fact voice. 'I've been up to my eyes in work.'

Whilst true, she'd have struggled to find space in her diary, had there been that all important invite, the ache in Jackie's heart had become unbearable. But never mind, her lady love was on the phone. And there was an explanation.

'Do you know what the trouble is?' Claudia began, knowing she must be forthright. She owed Jackie that, at least.

'No, do tell.' Jackie's heart was in her mouth. If it was the wretched accent, she'd get elocution. Any mortal thing she was happy to consider, to get their relationship off the ground.

'It's the distance between us.' This was as much as Claudia was willing to admit. The truth being she was still hurting from her previous let downs and was not ready to re-commit, by giving in to the stirrings this woman aroused in her. A true sister in the faith, too.

She was not in love with Jackie. Although knew it would go that way. If she let her heart rule her head. Jackie shot up one of her arrow requests. This one being for divine grace and wisdom. Because, if Claudia suspected the depth of Jackie's feelings, she may be scared off.

'Oh, I totally understand,' she therefore remarked then continued. 'Well, look. It's getting near the hols. We're going to be away the minute the schools finish, to brave the elements, whatever our English weather throws at us, to do a spot of camping. Call us crazy if you like. I'd have preferred a couple of weeks on a sun-drenched Mediterranean beach, I don't mind telling you. But our daughter's talked us into this latest adventure.' A few moments silence elapsed as Claudia pondered whether to give Jackie her thoughts on what a waste of precious time she considered either option. Bu was spared when Jackie piped up again.

'Well, thanks for putting me in the picture.' At which juncture, every ounce of her will was needed, to get off the line. It was Sunday evening.

'I must go,' she finally announced. 'I'm assisting Laura, best I'm able with her maths homework. Her father usually helps but he's on a call out.

With Claudia still silent, Jackie again took the lead.

'We'll just keep in touch. Shall we? Phone whenever you like. It does me a power of good hearing your voice.' This being the nearest Jackie dare venture towards admitting her true feelings.

Claudia had a good idea anyhow. It was adding to her concern. The last thing she wanted was to hurt Jackie. Or to let her down later.

'Very well. You go and help your daughter. I'm hopeless with numbers' she responded. 'Perhaps you'll be able to help me, one day. Charles reckons I give him nightmares with my spending when it comes to balancing the books.' She gave one of the funny little laughs Jackie was getting to know and which on this occasion, brought their conversation to a lighthearted end.

So that was it, Claudia reflected, as she replaced the receiver. For the early part of summer, anyhow. But, *yes*, she would be keeping in touch, had no intention of doing otherwise. She was just wary of getting carried away. That was all.

As for Jackie, despite her frustration, she was in a better frame of mind than she could possibly have been when, pulling up a chair at the kitchen table, she reined in her emotions to try help her daughter with an especially complex set of equations. They were, she reflected, as the session came to an end, a perfect example of the fragmented condition of her own heart. What the rest of the summer held she knew not.

But after saying goodnight to Laura, placed herself in the Hands of the One watching over the entire situation. Who she knew, unquestionably, *did*.

# CHAPTER 22

SEPTEMBER 1990
SEAPORT

The summer break brought much-needed refreshment with the holiday ending on a high note. They'd hired the biggest available tent and Ivan and Jackie had both taken the best part of three weeks leave. The tent which divided up into various sections had ensured relations did not become strained. The weather had been kind and a splendid time was had exploring every nook and cranny of the Isle of Wight. Candy had been in her element, sniffing out new territory and chasing her canine companions, every moment of the day.

On the first of September the family returned and, true to her word, Claudia had been in touch. First, with a *Welcome Home* card hidden in the middle of a pile of bills. The card had cheered her immensely but had served to drive home the message, things were destined to go forward at what, on Jackie's watch, was snail's pace.

By the fourth of September there was a few lines to which Jackie replied in kind. A plant arrived on the tenth for her birthday, bearing the message: *Fondest Thoughts C x.* A *Thank You* note had been dispatched by return. Signed simply: *Love Jackie x.*

Before Claudia finally made her mind up things could not go on in the same manner. It was a perfect late summer evening. She'd come away from St Cuth's with an inspired word from a lady preacher fresh in her mind. The message had been taken from

*Isaiah* and spoke of the need to let go of one's past and embrace the new thing God was waiting to do in a believer's life.

As Claudia strolled alongside the canal, her thoughts turned to Jackie. She was free, at last, from her past hurts. Arriving home to find Charles in his study and, having passed Tristram in the hall, on his way out, she'd gone to get her address book. Then, picking up the phone and making herself comfy on a rung of the stairs, she dialled Jackie's number. When Jackie answered on the third ring, Claudia didn't waste another moment.

'Hi. It's me.' She sounded unusually cheerful, a carefree lilt in her voice. 'How are you doing? What's your work schedule like for this week?' She tried to keep her tone casual despite some delectable stirrings in the pit of her tummy, at the sound of Jackie's voice. 'Is there a chance you can get up here?' She asked quickly. 'I've realized the summer's marching on.'

Jackie's heart raced as she fetched her diary. Please Lord, I *must* be free, she silently prayed. And upon checking, struggled to keep her voice steady.

'I'm off Friday,' she replied. Recalling gleefully how two cases had been cancelled. One of them after the defendant's solicitor had rung to say his client had gone into hospital. A clear window of opportunity which Jackie happily acknowledged as divine intervention. Her jubilation tempered only by a mild bout of regret some unsuspecting soul had needed hospitalization to provide that vital window. The other cancellation being down to human error and a double booking.

Therefore, if Friday suited Claudia, wild horses would not stop her pointing her prized motor in the direction of Kentley Manor. Once she'd consulted a map.

'Ah, sounds splendid,' Claudia enthused. 'I'll be able to fix us a nice little lunch.'

Jackie's heart was ready to burst. Providing nice little lunches and entertaining friends was how Claudia spent half her life, it hadn't taken Jackie long to realize. The other half being spent going round the shops or using her creativity within the church community. 'Sorry for the gap. I've been doing a spot of entertaining.' Or, 'apologies, I've been surrounded by fabric and needle and thread' were familiar introductions to her letters.

Jackie tightened her grip on the handset when she heard Claudia say. 'Even better. Why not stay the night? Unless you have plans for the weekend.'

She didn't re-check the diary for any weekend engagements. Laura was going to her friends after dance class, she already knew. And Ivan was on duty, he'd informed her, the previous day. Meaning all he'd need do was pick their daughter up, after work.

She carried the phone to the lounge and sat down for safety.

'No. I've nothing planned Saturday.'

'Wonderful. Get here soon as you're able.'

'Yes, of course.' Jackie responded. But Claudia had already hung up. She ached that very night for the kind of closeness enjoyed with her previous lovers, as she went to prepare the packed lunch Tristram had reminded her he would like. Then it

138

was nine thirty and bedtime. Being the early riser she was, she would be dressed at six thirty and could often be spotted by seven, cycling alongside the canal.

As her head hit the pillow, she was already making a series of adjustments for the week ahead. First, she would have to cancel that dental appointment scheduled for Friday afternoon. A couple of dodgy teeth causing a few twinges was not going to get in the way. Especially when she factored in the extra swim sessions. Not to mention more pedal pushing alongside the canal. If those excess pounds were going to be shed. Claudia's excitement continued to mount as fresh ideas sprang to mind. And, by the time an exceptionally warm summer came to an end, two lady friends would have turned into lovers.

Of this Claudia Elliott was now quite as certain, as she was of the fact, night follows day.

# CHAPTER 23

Jackie swore Millie, her little MX5 had sprouted wings that Friday as she sped along. By following the map Claudia had decided to drop her in the post, she had arrived in no time. Suddenly, there it was *Parklands*. Jackie spotted the brass name plate on the wooden gate. The house stood in a cul de sac, comprising the Elliott home along with four others. Parklands being the largest and standing back from the rest.

The gate was open awaiting her arrival. Jackie turned into the drive and parked a few strides from the front door. She stepped out of the car, taking her time to lock it up while gathering her composure. She'd just placed her finger on the bell when the oak paneled door flew open. Claudia was in perfect hostess mode.

'Why, hello. Do come in. Did you have a good journey?' Claudia had seen the car draw up while arranging, to her satisfaction, the sashes on the sitting room curtains.

'Yes, fine. Your map was so easy to follow. Thanks a bunch.'

Jackie's heart had done a somersault, at the sight of Claudia and at the sound of her voice. She was, nonetheless, feeling jaded, as she stepped inside. It hadn't been warm enough to have the hood down and her head throbbed with the concentration of driving.

'Let me take your coat.' Claudia helped Jackie out of a light raincoat. The forecast had given sunshine and showers. A bolt as of electric shot through Jackie at the brush of the two women's hands. Claudia felt it, too, as she took the coat to the cloakroom then returned to the hallway, looking stunning in a button through denim skirt and wine color silk waistcoat over a crisp cotton white shirt. Jackie's heart was pounding as her hostess nodded toward the lounge.

'Make yourself comfy. I expect you could do with a drink. Is it tea or coffee you prefer?'

'Oh either. Tea will be fine.' Jackie wasn't about to make a fuss. She sank into a stately looking armchair, then rummaged in her handbag bag for some Paracetamol. She put two aside to take with the drink. Having prayed and waited for this day for so long, the sheer exhilaration was threatening to overwhelm her.

'Sugar?' The voice resounded from the kitchen.

'No thank you' Jackie called back loudly.

Five minutes later and Claudia made her entrance, carrying a tray with a China teapot of a pretty, floral design with two matching cups and saucers and three plates. One of the plates bore two squares of flapjack and two shortbread fingers.

'I don't want to spoil your lunch, but you must be hungry. Did you stop at all?'

'No.'

She'd made a brief stop for the toilet but didn't say so.

'Ah, no wonder you made good time.'

'Well, yes. That and your splendid directions.'

Jackie had started out early after no more than a nibble of toast but still couldn't manage a thing.

Claudia helped herself to the flapjack. Jackie having refused all but the tea.

'I cannot resist flapjack. My favorite.' Claudia remarked before biting of a chunk then turning her head aside, wincing at the unpleasant sensation shooting down one side of her face.

Jackie failed to notice. She was lost in thought as she gazed around the room, taking in evidence of Claudia's creativity, wondering what a suitable topic of conversation might be. She'd refused Claudia's second offer of the goodies, not wanting to do further damage to her waistline. At half a stone heavier since the beginning of summer from comfort eating, she realized, when fretting over Claudia, on the occasions she hadn't kept in touch. Claudia was not what one would call sylph like either, despite her current fitness regime. Though at five foot ten and with her clever way of dressing, she could get away with a lot and still have the makings of a desirable woman. Anyhow, it was Claudia's self-description of 'tall and well made` which, after falling in love with her voice, had further fueled Jackie's interest. Sonia Bellinger was tall, large boned and creative. Amanda Samuels was above average height too and was possessed of a certain flair. It had led Jackie to the conclusion this was her type. And, with the lady in whose company she found herself today, their shared spirituality was the icing on the cake.

At just turned one, Jackie found herself sitting opposite her hostess around a circular pinewood table covered by a lemon broderie anglaise cloth.

142

With a supreme effort she managed to down a modest portion of the lunch. A green salad dotted with cherry tomatoes and a variety of peppers, accompanied by several other items adding color to the presentation; some Jackie could christen and a few she couldn't. Along with Quiche Lorraine and something she thought was Coronation Chicken. Then to follow came Ginger and Lime Cheesecake and Vanilla Ice Cream topped off with a wedge of lime. All homemade, Jackie didn't need telling. This lady was as adept in the kitchen as in most creative spheres of life.

The headache had subsided. But her heart was pounding, at the nearness of the one whom she had come to adore. And, in anticipation of what might happen next.

Her mind began wandering upstairs to what she was sure were very fine bedrooms. Her imagination began to run riot. What kind of lover would Claudia be? And, was she about to find out?

This was still a family home. A pair of large trainers and a hold-all with a squash racket poking out provided evidence. With Tristram, the likely owner of the equipment in college, however, and the Elliott husband at the office, the women were alone in the house.

'Don't worry if you can't finish it.' Claudia's gaze fell intent upon Jackie. As her guest pushed the cheesecake round and round on the willow patterned plate, she could see she was struggling and so remarked, 'I've provided rather a banquet. Haven't I?'

Jackie put down the spoon and laid a hand across her tummy.

'Yes, and I'm so sorry. I can't manage any more. It's delicious. But my stomach's shrunk since doing a spot of dieting.'

A modicum of tact was essential. Claudia had gone to a great deal of effort and Jackie was concerned things did not get off on the wrong foot.

'Oh, leave the rest.' Claudia responded and, getting up, moved in much closer. When she put out a hand to touch Jackie's forearm, Jackie's hopes rose sky high.

The two had yet to experience any outward demonstrations of affection. Such as the hugs of greeting which were part of the Fosters' Christian friendships. Claudia's hugs and kisses, she surmised, were maybe the kind reserved for those she was in some sort of close relationship with.

'Do come upstairs. There's something I'm dying to show you.' Claudia issued the sudden invitation, standing by the door leading to the hallway.

*This*, Jackie told herself, is IT. Her stomach lurched so violently she became convinced she'd be sick. Before a morsel of the food, she'd managed to force down had digested.

The two women then climbed the wide, open staircase. Claudia leading with Jackie one step behind.

'Come along.' Claudia beckoned Jackie toward the doorway of one of the bedrooms. 'In here,' she spoke softly, standing aside.

'Er, could I use the bathroom?' Jackie asked.

'Of course.' Claudia replied with a knowing smile.

As Jackie headed that way, her hostess disappeared into a room containing a double bed. Along with the hidden mystery.

Jackie emerged from the bathroom, having quickly freshened up best she could. She was feeling pathetically shy as she went to join Claudia who was still on her feet. She's bashful too, and wants to begin things slowly, was running through Jackie's mind as the two stood facing each other. Before Claudia broke the silence.

'Well, here we are,' she announced boldly, turning toward the wall to whip off a dust cover, from a large item hanging there. Then Jackie was given the surprise of her life as the unveiling right next to where her hostess was standing took place, to reveal *the* most jaw dropping piece of artwork, in the form of a collage. The younger woman stood transfixed, her round eyes widening further, as Claudia's beam stretched from ear to ear.

'All down to the efforts of St Cuth's junior section,' she remarked. A note of triumph in her voice. 'I got them to collect the flowers and foliage themselves, then helped with the drying and pressing. There's refurbishment going on at the church so it's here for safe keeping. Tell me.' She went on, continuing to beam. 'What do you think?'

Oh, tickety tickety, *tickety* boo. How terribly, *terribly* nice, was going through Jackie's mind as, open mouthed she gazed at the display. Then lowered her head at her failure to be as impressed as she might. Had it not been for her aching need.

Exactly *when* was the main action going to start? The collage was awesome. There was no doubt about it. A work of pure delight. She hadn't driven all those miles though, to give an assessment on the creative genius of a bunch of Sunday school children. If she had, their efforts would have chalked up ten and a half marks out of ten.

'Well yes. Definitely. You must have super clever kids at your church.' Jackie replied with all the diplomacy she could muster. Considering the state which she was in. So on fire with desire.

'I'll show you your room now,' was to be Claudia's next bright suggestion. 'You're staying the night, I take it. Have you left your things in the car?'

Jackie had left her overnight bag in the boot. Being too uptight to give it a thought, upon arrival.

'Yep. I'll fetch it and start back tomorrow morning' she replied, trying not to let the tone of her voice reflect her disappointment.

Oh, what's the use? This woman's not sure *what* she wants was flooding her mind. How could she, if *half* as turned on as Jackie had been for the past two hours, how on earth could she stay so cool, calm, and collected?

'Perfect.' Claudia maintained that selfsame nonchalant air. 'You get your bag. Then how about a walk? It promises to be a pleasant afternoon. No sign of the rain which was forecast which had me thinking of taking you into our amazing shopping center. But that can wait.'

Although Jackie had no clue, Claudia was becoming less in control of the situation, by the minute. The shopping trip having paled into insignificance. All she longed for was to take Jackie in her arms.

As her guest returned, she lingered in the doorway of the room ready and prepared for her. Glancing down at the bed then at Jackie, her back to Claudia, arranging her things, she had to fight not to make that first move. To perch on the edge of the bed. From where she could pull Jackie down into their first lovers 'embrace, before helping each other undress and slip between the crisp cotton sheets. She somehow managed to restrain herself. Not quite the moment, she decided.

This unfolding romance was vital enough to her, as well as the other person involved, to want to do things right. When this partnership came into its own, it would be no quick fling which would burn itself out, Claudia sensed deep within. Besides which, she was dog tired, having been up since crack of dawn.

'Well, why not? Let's have a walk.' Jackie said brightly. Striving not to allow her plain-speaking Yorkshire way of handling such a delicate situation come to the fore. Because if it did, she was sure to say something she would later regret.

How long though? For goodness sake. How long was all the teasing and tantalizing destined to go on? Especially here, with the prospect of a partner whom Jackie had thought to be on the same wavelength.

If the next few hours didn't bring a result. And, to coin a phrase of her late mother's, Jackie Foster thought she was sure to go quite *stone mad*.

# CHAPTER 24

In the event, Jackie was amazed how the rest of the day flew by. A couple of hours spent meandering along the canal bank was where the women discovered more of each other's background. Details emerged of how both came to faith. Claudia, Jackie learned, was brought up a strict Baptist and had put that down, at first, as the reason for her lack of interest in boys when her school friends started dating. It was as time went on; she began to sense she was different.

The two women discussed all manner of things as they rested at intervals on the wooden benches provided by Kentley Council. Claudia put an arm around Jackie's shoulders each time they needed a break. Just as on that first Oxford date. Then she suggested they visit a local café where Jackie found enough appetite to share a toasted fruit teacake with Claudia. And, by the time they got back, Jackie was left thinking Kentley Manor new town might be just her kind of place.

Once indoors, Claudia went to get Charles some dinner, inviting her guest to make herself comfy in the sitting room. Jackie sat, staring blankly at the TV screen, as the newscaster churned out the depressing headlines. A leader somewhere in the Middle East was about to invade someone else's territory and threatening any resistance would lead to bloodshed.

Claudia came through as the local news was starting.

'Oh,' she announced. 'Charles will be in any minute.' This left Jackie wondering if to stay put. Or whether the statement was a cue to make herself scarce. Claudia's next remark brought clarity.

'He'll disappear into his study straight after his meal. He's never finished with the job.'

Jackie expressed surprise.

'Really. Even at the weekend?'

'Yes. He can hardly get through the door Fridays; his briefcase is often that bulging.

'He sounds a busy man.' Jackie didn't know what to make of it all.

'He is. Anyhow, it'll keep him occupied the rest of the evening.' Claudia went on.

'Ah,' responded Jackie.

'Yes. And Tristram goes to his current girlfriends Fridays, from college. So, with my second daughter on holiday and my eldest having flown the nest, as I'm sure I've told you, we'll have the house to ourselves. Don't fret.'

It was sufficient to fill Jackie with renewed hope their day had not reached its conclusion.

At five to seven Charles walked in, and after dumping the briefcase, took off his jacket then went through to eat without even noticing their guest.

'You're late, Charles. I was beginning to worry.' Claudia popped her head round the dining room door as Charles was pouring himself a glass of wine.

'Yes. I called in at Stacy Brompton's. Needed to get my poor old tool fixed. Hopeless, it was, trying to get any satisfaction on that dresser. You said so yourself when you walked in on me at the height of my frustration.'

'Did I?'

'Well, yes. You caught me huffing and puffing and uttering the odd swear word. Without lending so much as a hand.'

Their voices reverberated from kitchen to dining room and through to the lounge, leaving Jackie quite bemused. Whatever was Charles on about and what sort of marriage did this couple have? Furthermore, if she didn't make her excuses and leave right away what kind of set up might she be getting herself into?

With no more time to reflect Charles, having finished his dinner, strode into the sitting room. He looked normal enough anyhow, was Jackie's first impression. Tall, slim, with an intelligent air about him, and the most extraordinary eyes. Inky blue and intense. Yet with a mischievous twinkle.

Claudia came in from the kitchen at the moment her husband realized they had a guest.

'Charles, I would like you to meet Jackie. Jackie, this is Charles.'

'How do you do?' Charles proffered a hand. Jackie was about to get to her feet as she held out hers in return. 'No, stay where you are.' Charles stooped to give Jackie a brief handshake.

'Have you come far?' He didn't recall Claudia mentioning they'd anyone staying. Though was happy, nonetheless, to welcome Jackie, along with every other woman in his wife's life. All with their various roles and functions.

'I've driven up from Seaport.'

'She's staying the night.'

The two women chorused in unison.

That sounds about right, Charles reflected. Confident he was getting an accurate picture. Once he knew their pretty little guest was of the overnight kind.

'Well, enjoy your stay Jean... sorry, Jackie, wasn't it, you said? I'm sure Claudia's looking after you. But if you need anything, just ask. Goodnight.'

At this, Charles sauntered off, whistling what Jackie swore were a few bars of '*Love is in the Air*,' as the study door slammed shut.

Oh well, Jackie mused. Whatever sort of marriage this couple had, who was she to question?

The only thing plaguing her mind was when two lady friends were going to turn into lovers. Could it happen before the day ended? And before that fancy looking cuckoo clock hung in the hall tweeted midnight.

When Claudia re-appeared and placed a pile of magazines on the coffee table, Jackie's hopes reached an all-time low.

At quarter to nine, after clearing away in the kitchen and, in the same polite manner extended to all her guests, Claudia excused herself.

'That walk was much needed, but it completely did me in, I'm afraid. However, the whole house is yours to enjoy. Feel free to take a shower; a bath, or anything else you might like. And do help yourself to a nightcap. There's hot chocolate and a selection of teas. Oh, and there's the rest of the shortbread in the cupboard above the toaster,' she added. Then bid Jackie goodnight and turned towards the stairs.

Jackie picked up a *She* magazine.

'Goodnight,' she replied loud and clear. As the mag fell open on a page headed *Falling in Love turned Fory.* Subtitled *The Pleasures and Pitfalls.*

She closed the magazine and put it down. Way past perusing instructions and perfectly willing to learn as she went along.

She doesn't fancy me. Not one iota. The police wife petulantly thought. I've come all this way. I must go back tomorrow. And the way things are looking, I'm not a jot nearer having this woman as my lover than the first time we clapped eyes on each other. She recalled Charles's words. 'If you need anything, ask.' What a joke. What a sick, cruel joke this was turning out to be. She'd just about had enough.

While Claudia's reflections were of a totally different kind. When, despite her exhaustion, she lay awake a very long time. Restless and filled with longings. Longings for her and her new lady to act out the scenes imprinting themselves on her mind.

Oh yes, that would be so *very* nice, was to become her last thought.at the end of what had, in her estimation, anyway, been a most pleasant day.

# CHAPTER 25

## LATE SEPTEMBER 1990
## PARKLANDS

The day had begun around seven thirty with Charles having left for a Men's Breakfast; a Christian gathering he attended one Saturday each month. It happened to be this very one. God had, at the eleventh hour, arranged all things well.

Jackie had been sitting up in bed, Bible in one hand and Scripture notes in the other, when there was a tap on the door and the clink of cups. Followed by the words 'Can I come in?'

'Yes' Jackie yelled, putting the reading to one side, telling herself to expect nothing beyond what sounded like the promise of a very welcome cuppa.

Claudia entered in her plum color satin nightgown, passed Jackie her drink and then perched on the edge of the bed with her own cup and saucer.

Gazing down upon her guest, she could barely keep her hand steady.

'Did you sleep well?' She asked.

'Yes not bad.' Jackie responded. The truth being she'd retired at ten after taking a shower to try and relax. But had tossed and turned till around three. Tormented by unfulfilled longings.

'I'll finish this then I'll join you.' Claudia spoke between sips of tea as Jackie almost spilled hers over the floral print bedspread.

Having drunk up, Claudia took Jackie's cup and turning back the covers, got in beside her. As they lay face to face, Claudia lifted her nightie then Jackie's, too, above their chests.

Jackie gasped at the warmth and softness of sensation, upon finding herself enfolded in a mummy bear kind of embrace. The lovers kissed. Tenderly at first before a torrent of passion overtook them. Immediately the kiss ended, Claudia sat up and hauled her nightie over her head. Flinging it to the floor, she helped Jackie off with hers.

Jackie gazed with wonder at Claudia's ample, milky white breasts. Before becoming lost in a warm sensual sea of delight. It was so exquisite, so perfect. Ripples of pleasure turned to ecstasy as their acts of deep intimacy gathered pace.

The chemistry between them was simply superb. And *yes,* the love was there. On the older woman's side, too. Claudia was left in no doubt as she held Jackie close then sat up to look into the radiance of her new lover's brightly flushed face. While not forgetting to thank the God Whom they worshiped. For the woman lying at her side and what He had allowed to take place.

And that is how it began. Two Christian women. Each committed to their faith and to their husbands and families. Yet, with such a burning need. A need the church could neither condone nor relate to. There was only their Maker, the Good Lord, Himself Who understood. And Who they trusted to guide them. Whatever lay ahead.

'Happy Darling?' Claudia continued to gaze upon Jackie as they lay close together. In the afterglow of that first glorious encounter.

Jackie was so ecstatic; it took what seemed an eternity for her to respond.

'Not half,' she eventually replied. 'Though with one tiny query I'd love to resolve before I point Millie towards the south coast.'

'Go on then.'

Claudia was both puzzled and intrigued.

'Who's this Stacy woman? Is Charles having an affair? And how does that make you feel?'

Claudia gave a hearty laugh and swung her feet to the floor.

'*Stacy Brompton*, my precious, is an industrial estate between here and the railway station.'

'*Industrial Estate?*'

'Yes, Charles calls in there when he needs to get a household tool, or some other item repaired.'

Jackie broke into a giggle. It was exactly the right kind of moment to bring an unforgettable stay to its end.

So, it was with joy she sped off.

There were tricky times ahead. For sure. Right at that moment, however, her heart was bursting with love and a fresh sense of self-worth. Along with a fulfillment she never knew existed. She switched on the radio in perfect time to hear Dusty belt out...

*Just a little loving*
*Early in the morning*
*Beats a cup of coffee*
*For starting off the day*
*Just a little loving*
*Makes you wake up feeling*
*Good things are coming your way.*

And by the time she reached Seaport, Jackie Rose Foster was feeling on top of the world.

# CHAPTER 26

'You've what? I can see I'll have to get my hearing tested, after all.'

Jackie scowled. 'How do you mean?'

'I thought you said you'd taken a weekend job'. Claudia gave a shrill laugh. 'Put me right darling. What should I have heard?'

'You heard right. And all a case of needs must.'

'Well, when are we going to meet?' Claudia was aghast. 'It's hard enough, making that long trip, as time goes by. I'm not getting any younger. And I'm worried. Where *is* Ivan, anyway?'

'He's gone and left me. If you must know.'

'Ah. Gone as deputy to Hounslow.'

Jackie was speechless as she began the hunt for her slippers and as Claudia blundered on.

'Come tell me more.' She patted the empty space next to her on the sofa. 'It can't be financial, surely. Unless…'

Jackie cut in. 'Unless what?'

'Well, unless Ivan's been demoted?'

The women had been together four years. Both Ivan and Charles had been most accommodating. Neither wanted to see their marriage crumble. So, had both with good grace, gone the extra mile where necessary, to help the situation along. Charles had become increasingly involved outside the UK on work-related business. Jackie, on all such occasions, would take a day or two of her annual leave and drive up to Parklands. Ivan, likewise, would make himself scarce, whenever Claudia came to Seaport. As for Laura, a teenager now, she welcomed every opportunity to go stay with friends.

The women were still very much in love. What was more, life had treated them kindly. Until the relationship was dealt its first blow.

Jackie had picked Claudia up at the station on her way home from work. Claudia was making them a cup of tea when Jackie broke the news. But the older woman with her ostrich like mentality would bury her head in the sand whenever a crisis was looming. It exasperated Jackie and they were heading toward the kind of row they'd never had. But Jackie couldn't find the grace to keep stumm.

'As I said, he's left me. And there's no wonder. *Is* there?' She yelled, abandoning the search for her slippers, thinking Candy would be sure to have hidden them, as was her favorite trick.

She went barefoot to fetch the brew. Claudia patted the vacant cushion beside her again. Jackie chose to ignore the invite and plonked down in an armchair. Glad to have good reason to shout.

'It's tele sales,' she continued. 'Three evenings and every other weekend. There's a mortgage and bills to pay here.' She gave a sigh of exasperation. Candy barked furiously at the sound of Jackie's raised voice. Laura had been home, fed and walked her, before the women got in. Then gone to her best friend's house for the night.

Jackie got up to release the dog from imprisonment and to check if the slippers were in her basket. Not caring a jot about Claudia's distaste for the animal. Candy went to lay directly in front of her and gave an enormous grunt, as Jackie continued to bellow.

'The extra job's the only way. Unless you can think of something.' It was going to be tough; the younger woman knew. Even with her faith to sustain her and, despite her love for this woman, Jackie was at the end of her tether. Claudia, having gaped open mouthed, throughout Jackie's tirade, spoke again.

'*Me* think of something. Well no. But why should I? What has any of this got to do with me? And you can't be going to work Sundays. That can never be right.'

Jackie's round cheeks burned with anger.

'It's got *everything* to do with you. And with us. For heaven's sake.'

Ivan had found the decency to explain his leaving was not totally related to the extra person in their marriage. He'd unresolved issues of his own. Needed time to go find himself, had been his way of putting things. It was ludicrous however, for Claudia to eliminate their relationship from the equation.

Jackie gulped down the tea and, slippers retrieved, shuffled into the kitchen. She was sloshing salad items round and round endlessly in a colander under the cold tap to try and dispel her anger. Normally, they would enjoy a simple meal before relaxing in each other's company, watching TV, perhaps, or listening to music, then retiring early to bed.

160

There was nothing normal about tonight's get together though and it was gone seven when they sat down to eat. To the accompaniment of a strained silence. The dog got up and went to sit next to Claudia, emitting a huge snort which, in doggy speak translated 'don't forget me and I'm starving.' It was the last straw. Claudia put down her knife and fork after just one mouthful.

'Look, darling, I'm exhausted, too.' She stayed infuriatingly calm. While at the bottom of her, Jackie was spoiling for a row. The sort of barney they'd never had. Their relationship was being sorely tested as Claudia went on.

'The meal's fine. I'm just too all in to eat. I'll go have a lie down then ring Charles. He's sure to come and fetch me in the morning. The train will be heaving, being bank holiday.' Claudia's face bore a hint of apology as Jackie took fright. She so needed this woman. And, despite her anger, did not know how she'd cope if she lost her. She put down her cutlery, too, then Claudia, without another word, got up and, after walking round to Jackie's side of the table, clasped her left hand in both of her own.

'Look. Let's not spoil what we've been blessed with for so long. And can continue to enjoy. If we work at it.' She let go of Jackie's hand and sat down beside her. 'I think we should cut our losses for once. Why didn't you phone the minute Ivan went? I'd have come straight away.' Claudia searched Jackie's face. Her lover was beginning to look ten years older already.

'I was hoping he'd be back after a few days.' Jackie replied with a sigh. 'Haven't a clue where he is. Just insists he's OK if I do manage to speak to him at the station.' Her face brightened momentarily as she went on. 'But I'm praying he'll be back before Christmas. For Laura's sake, at least.'

Claudia pulled up the nearest chair to reach out and put an arm around Jackie.

'If you'd given me warning it wouldn't have been such a bombshell. Never mind. We can't always get things right.' She got up and stroked Jackie's neat crop of ash blonde hair then bent to kiss the top of her head, before making her way upstairs.

Jackie finished what she could of the tasty lamb chop, out of the two she'd grilled to accompany some new potatoes, along with a sweet and crunchy salad. She shunted the remains of her meal into the bin. Then put Claudia's portion aside. Supposedly for Ivan. Before realizing afresh her husband was not coming home for that, or any other meal.

After nearly twenty-five years, the new situation was taking some getting used to. It was only ten days since her husband had walked out.

She loaded the dishwasher, then traumatized, as well as overworked, burst into tears. For the first time since Claudia Elliott had come into her life, Jackie was counting the cost.

Claudia could not or would not leave Charles. The Foster wife had known from the start. The Elliott husband was in control of both his marriage and financial affairs. And though exceedingly charming on the surface, could hold very tight purse strings when it suited him to do so. Which neither his faith commitment, nor anything else was allowed to get in the way of.

So where, Jackie pondered, did they go from here? Could their journeys continue along the same path?

She prayed desperately for a way forward. Which would enable them to travel this rocky stretch she was now forced to negotiate, still *together.*

# CHAPTER 27

Claudia didn't get to phone Charles in the end. Jackie had taken a call from him after his wife had gone for her early night. He had an emergency meeting with the London Met, due to a terrorist attack on the Kentley to London line, Charles had gone on to explain and Jackie had popped a note next to Claudia's Bible. Upon finding her sleeping.

Then, as Saturday dawned with Laura having returned from her overnight stay to get Candy to accompany her on a camping trip, Jackie had good reason to thank the Good Lord the two women had awoken in the same house.

She was just coming to when there was the familiar rattle of cups and a gentle tap on the door.

'Come in,' Jackie shouted.

'Oh, how nice.' She eased herself up and took the brew from her lover. A decent night's sleep had refreshed her. Nothing had changed. But she was at peace, as Claudia set her drink down before slipping into bed beside her.

'My own precious darling. I'm sorry about last night. For what happened. Truly I am. You need my support more than ever. Don't you? And thanks for the note. I can't let these awful bombings stop me. I need to get here somehow.' Her hand began to search out Jackie under her nightie.

'We must pray for all the families of those poor people affected though.'

'Yes, course.' Jackie murmured. Melting at her lover's touch.

It was so reminiscent of that first Parklands encounter when Claudia had brought her a morning cuppa. They'd come a long way since. Yet nothing had changed. Except their love had grown deeper.

Claudia retrieved her hand to take Jackie in her arms. She traced the worry lines appearing on her face.

For, although time had dimmed what had been an unstoppable passion, the same vital spark remained. Each time they came together in their own special way.

It had been no passing fancy. This was an act of two women who genuinely loved one another.

Sunday had begun with Claudia paying only her second visit to Jackie's Community church. They'd sped there and back with the roof down and Claudia's hair flying in the wind. Once home, the older woman had insisted Jackie rest while she did them a roast. After which they'd taken a long walk. Then, with Laura and the dog out of the way, the two women had laid in each other's arms all night. Jackie had fallen asleep at Claudia's breast. Next thing she knew it was eight o'clock and, once Claudia had checked the trains, time to take her lady love to the station.

'I don't know how I'm going to part from you.' Claudia leaned over Jackie to bestow a few final caresses all over her, struggling to let go of the moment. And it was to be Jackie, with her strength renewed, who took the lead.

'Well, let's be thankful for what we have *had*. Think what we would've missed. If Charles hadn't been stopped from fetching you.' She swung her legs out of bed, leaving Claudia with no option but to do likewise. And prepare for the journey home.

They had reached a crossroads, however. Both women realized. As Jackie dropped Claudia off at Castlehampton Central. And, as the train pulled on to the platform.

'Bye, my love.' Claudia's eyes locked with Jackie's. Then once onboard, she turned and waved.

'Till next time.' Jackie mouthed the words, as the train pulled away.

And there would be a next time, And a next and a next, Jackie knew. At whatever cost, Jackie was in this for the long haul. All she could do was trust, hope and pray Claudia Frances Elliott was, too.

# CHAPTER 28

'It's me. Put Laura on, will yer?'

Ivan's call took Jackie by surprise. They hadn't spoken in weeks. He would simply toot to announce his arrival on the fortnightly visits to see their daughter. Laura would jump into the four-by-four, and off they'd go into town. To the cinema or maybe the bowling alley, or the park if they'd taken Candy.

After spending some of half-term with Ivan though, Laura had come back with news.

'I won't be seeing much of dad for a while. He's busy and I'm not that bothered. His place's grotty. I'd rather be with Ben. Their house is huge. His sister's a good laugh, as well.'

Laura wasn't yet fifteen. Ben was eighteen. The amount of time they were spending together was an added anxiety for Jackie. So, Ivan's call was both timely and welcome.

She was off to Claudia's at the end of the main break. But her and Laura were going to be alone Christmas day. Meaning Jackie was feeling even less festive than usual. It was the time she missed their old friends most and she'd made an excuse not to go to her works dinner. Hardly anyone knew Ivan had left and she couldn't face it.

'Oh, hi.' She tried to sound casual. 'Laura's in her room. Getting ready to do some carol singing.'

Jackie had just got in from working her last shift before the Christmas break.

'I've persuaded her to join the youngsters at the Lantern, but it's taken some doing, seeing she thinks herself too grown up.

In the short pause which followed, Jackie felt the tears pricking the back of her eyes.

'I thought you'd abandoned her. As well as me.'

'Have I heck. Don't talk daft. It's been murder. Aye. Literally murder. Always t'same in front er Christmas. Two armed robberies near 'ere. Yer must have heard summat on t'news.'

Nothing's changed, Jackie consoled herself. Ivan thought all she did was listen to every news bulletin that filled the airwaves. The reality being, she came face to face with the folks his team had apprehended, the minute they arrived at court.

Anyhow, Jackie didn't believe her husband's excuse for not having time for Laura. He'd found consolation elsewhere. That, Jackie suspected, was the real reason. Her suspicion heightened by remarks from Laura, at the end of another outing, when Jackie had asked if they'd had a good time.

'No, there was a horrid smell of cheap perfume in dad's car. When I asked him about it he said it was my imagination.' Laura had replied.

Oh, what a mess it all was. And how Jackie wished at that moment, she didn't have need of Claudia Elliott in her life.

'Well, is she there then?' Ivan bawled. After his bulletin on life at the station. 'I can't stay on t'blower all night.'

Jackie was stalling for time and choking back the tears. She didn't expect they would help.

'Laura's gone. I'll get her to call you.' She wasn't sure, hadn't been to look. But was experiencing a sudden urge to grab Ivan's attention, all to herself.

'She's gone, has she? Well tell her to ring mi.' Next came a loud slurping noise.

He must have made himself a pot of his Yorkshire brew or felt need of something stronger before picking up the phone ran through Jackie's mind, before he spoke again.

'I'd best be off. You an' me said all there is to say before I decided to hop it.' There was, to be heard another huge slurp. 'I take it you're coping wi what I'm sending. Money wise I mean.' Whereby, came a thud and 'Aw, bloody hell.' Then silence while he rubbed his head and recovered something from underneath the phone shelf.

'That's t'waste of a pot er decent tea an' a bump t'size of a duck egg on mi left temple,' he finally confessed. Before returning to the matter in hand. 'Yer'll 'av to manage. I can't send any more.'

Ivan was transferring a regular amount into their still open joint account. It fell far short though, of providing for the lifestyle they'd been used to. His wife took a deep breath.

'Yep, coping in a fashion. I've no choice. Have I?' She didn't mention the part-time work, at realizing she'd have to give it up in the new year. If her main job and Laura weren't to suffer in other significant ways.

'This is not all about money though. Is it?' She persisted.

'What's it about then? Let's have it.'

'Well, no. You're the one who walked out. You tell me.'

'I told yer, I'd reached t'end er mi tether. An` it's not just to do wi you and Mrs fancy pants. Though, I don't know how Charles has put up wi what's gone on. Christian, or not, a fella has himsen to think of. That bloke's a saint. Or there's summat we don't know.'

Jackie's distress turned to anger. Her husband was stubborn as a mule.

'Well, if it's not about my issues, what *is* it about? If you won't meet and talk things through, it's game over. Think of Laura, *please* Ivan. If you can't bear to do anything else for me.'

Jackie took a few deep breaths.

'How are you spending Christmas anyway?'

'Workin.' Till we've got this lot we're lookin` for behind bars.'

There was a pause. Then, as Jackie was about to speak, he was off again.

'Hey, an` I'm not talkin` t'sort they go leanin` on to sink their pints, to find enough bravado to do what they must, to put some decent grub on t'table. If this bloody if this government hadn't...'

Jackie cut in.

'I'm losing you. I thought you needed to get off the line. Not start a political debate. You're not working Christmas day. Are you? You hardly ever work Christmas day. Unless it's a call out.'

170

'What's it matter? I've mi plans. Off to church, I'll be trotting Christmas morning. There's a Baptist's near where I'm living.'

'Oh.'

'Aye. I'm a Baptist, at heart. It's where I went as a kid. This Holy Spirit stuff's getting us nowhere. Well, getting me nowhere, any road.'

He'd been invited to spend Christmas with a woman. Jackie was right. Despite his faith commitment, her husband had sought consolation elsewhere. Jodie Chambers was a divorcee with a young son. She didn't belong to the faith, however, and his heart wasn't in it. He was planning to tell her it was over by the New Year.

'Oh, Ivan. We all feel like that, at times. Course it was getting us somewhere. All the prayer times. Not to mention other activities we were part of as a team. Anyway, think of your daughter. Laura needs you.' Jackie took another deep breath then went on, 'Why don't you come round for Christmas dinner? She's spending far too much time in the company of an older boy. The situation needs a fatherly eye casting over it.'

'Is she sleeping wi him? It's against t'law. I'll have him.'

'I hope not.' Jackie was appalled Ivan could entertain the thought. But knew she was on the right track to tear down his defenses. 'Look I must go, too.'

The sound of Laura's footsteps told her she hadn't left. What she wasn't aware of, was the fact she'd been listening from the landing. What she did realize was, she needed to get their daughter motivated. Otherwise, she'd skip the carol singing and get on the phone to Ben.

Jackie took the bull by the horns.

'Go to your service. I'll give church a miss, Christmas morning. I'm going to the midnight one, on Christmas Eve. 'Go to your service. Then why not come here. We're having leg of pork and a huge side of ham. None of the dry old turkey you complain about every year.'

A bit of pork was Ivan's favorite. Although, the fact was, she planned to do her big food shop the following day.

The next silence proved long enough to give rise to suspicion the digestive juices were beginning to flow. His next request brought confirmation.

'Apple an` cranberry sauce. An` plenty er them little bangers wrapped i` bacon, pig's...pig's ear or summat.'

'Oh, you mean pigs in blankets?'

'Aye, plenty er them. An` some er yer homemade stuffing. None er t'crap out er a packet.

'Yep. No prob.'

At which point Jackie could have sworn came the smacking of lips.

'Okey dokey. Yer on. See yer at one. Tell Laura I'll be seeing yer both soon. Hey. An` one last thing. Don't forget t'brandy sauce. Yer knows I can't entertain mi Christmas pud without it.'

There was a click, and the line went dead.

Jackie put down the phone with a triumphant grin. It might not be such a bad Christmas after all, she reflected. Sinking to her knees in the hallway thanking the Good Lord for His intervention. At the

very moment, too, Laura bolted downstairs, Candy
hot on her heels, barking wildly.

'Bye, mum. I'm off. What the heck are you doing
on your knees?' Her daughter asked with mock
surprise, as Candy gave Jackie's face a huge lick.

'My dad's coming home for Christmas,' were the
first words Laura spoke, after stepping into her
friend's dad's car. To be driven off and sing her
heart out, around Castlehampton's rather grand tree.

# CHAPTER 29

CHRISTMAS DAY 1994
SEAPORT

Months of relying on a pierce film and peel back diet meant Ivan's Christmas dinner had gone down a treat. Especially seeing the one with whom Ivan had indulged in a brief fling had taken umbrage, at his refusal to spend Christmas with her.

Candy had settled herself at Ivan's feet, reluctant to move after her share of the festive fayre. Leaving Jackie with no choice but to hook the lead onto her collar then drag her to the door, so father and daughter could clear away. When Jackie returned, all the better for a good dose of fresh air and some exercise, Laura was on pins.

'Mum, I've asked dad if he'll stay the night.' She piped up. 'He says he'd love to. But I have to OK things with you.' This was before Jackie had even taken off her wet coat and as Candy shook off the snowflakes beginning to fall.

Ivan had retreated to the sitting room while Laura loaded the dishwasher. He was standing staring out the window at the snow, reflecting that they hadn't seen a white Christmas during their time in the south. But that it looked likely they were going to see one now.

Jackie opened and shut her mouth without a sound coming out. Eager to take off her coat, she went to hang it over the kitchen door and yanked off her boots.

Laura was rooted to the spot, awaiting Jackie's return.

'Aw, go on mum. Look at it.' She nodded toward the kitchen window.

It was decision time, Jackie knew. Despite lots of forced jollity as they exchanged pressies, the situation was fragile.

If she asked Ivan to stay, it raised questions concerning the terms upon which he was being invited. On the other hand, if she turned her husband out of the marital home on a snowy Christmas night, it would surely mean the end of their marriage.

'Oh Lord. How shall I play this?' Jackie pleaded for divine help. She thought of darling Claudia with whom she'd only been able to share a discreet call, many hours ago. Then she cast her mind back to the freedom they'd enjoyed since Ivan's departure.

With all this going round in her head, Ivan sauntered back into the kitchen. As she retreated to fill the kettle, Laura began to dry Candy down with an old towel. She broke off to look up at her father.

'I've asked mum if you can stay. Have you seen the snow?'

'Aye. I've seen it. Not fit to turn a dog out. Is it, our Candy?' Ivan shot a glance toward Candy, before transferring his gaze inn the direction of his wife's back, as she brewed the tea. 'And what did mum say?'

Laura was getting ready to press Jackie for an answer. But there was no need.

'Stay. Course you must stay.' Her mother responded. The words out before she could stop them. 'You're not on duty tomorrow then?'

'Hope not.' Ivan replied, giving Laura a wink accompanied by a thumbs up then deciding he'd best check his mobile. Returning with the gadget, he went to sit on the lounge sofa, as Jackie re-appeared carrying the tea tray. The women were then allowed to satisfy their curiosity, fiddling around, pressing various buttons on the strange looking block of metal, while they all drank their tea.

Hours later, once Jackie had rustled up light snacks, the three of them settled down for a game of Trivial Pursuit. After which it was Laura's turn to wrap up and give Candy her last walk.

Then, oh dear, Jackie felt her heart sink as Laura, having re-appeared and dried Candy down again announced she was off to her room. Unable to wait another second to try out the music center Ivan had, in the end, decided to give her. Along with a crisp ten-pound inside a card bearing the message: *'Happy Christmas to our wonderful daughter. Lots of love Mum and Dad XX.*

Candy bounded upstairs after Laura as the inspector went to the bathroom to freshen up. Intent on making the most of what was left of the day.

'Well, that leaves we two Mrs Foster.' Ivan had sat himself next to his wife on the sofa. 'We won't be seeing either er them again tonight. If t'racket comin' from up there's owt to go by.'

Laura had managed to unpack the center and was testing the tape deck out on a festive number her dad had included. When Candy set up a howl, to the

176

accompaniment of some artist's version of *I wish it could be Christmas Every Day.*

The couple had listened together, for once, to the news. Then it was nine twenty-five on a snowy Christmas night.

'Shall we leave goggle-box on for Morecambe and Wise? Or shall we make our own entertainment? Seein' t'night's still young.'

Ivan had found himself unable to resist. Here he was. Alone with his wife. First time in several months. There were issues to be thrashed out. It was true. But Christmas night was not the time for such dialogue to take place.

Jackie yawned. She didn't have to pretend. The day had left her drained and physically exhausted.

'The night might be young. But I'm not,' she countered. 'TV sounds perfect then a prayer together'll be nice. If I can keep my eyes open.'

Ivan shot up and went to the kitchen, returning with a bottle of Chardonnay he'd brought and hidden at the back of the fridge's soft drinks shelf. Though, only occasional drinkers these days, Ivan knew this to have once been Jackie's tipple. He went to the display cabinet, poured, and then handed her a glass of the wine.

'Here, mi love.'

He had no intention of getting either of them – what was the word? He'd even forgotten that after years of sobriety. Sizzled. That was it. Or, maybe sozzled. Yes, sozzled had a better ring to it. Ivan had no intention of getting them both sozzled. Just a little tipsy should do the trick. He clinked his glass against the one in his wife's hand.

'To us and to the Good Lord. And to our bunch of three...well four, if we include that hound, at One, Blenheim Drive.'

Ivan became glassy eyed before he'd touched more than a drop. Jackie sipped slowly, too, from her glass, as he joined her again on the sofa.

The combination of alcohol and the antics of the pair on TV had her laughing so much she felt herself relax. She was in hysterics at one point. Until she felt Ivan's arm slide around her shoulders, and the mood of the moment slip away. She put down her glass and yawned. Loudly.

'Finish that if you like. It's been a great day, but I'm whacked.' She got up soon as the programme ended, forcing Ivan's arm off her. He took a swig of the wine and after draining his glass, tipped the remains of Jackie's into it. His wife spoke again.

'I'm going up to bed now. Switch everything off. Then why not come join me.'

The words flew off her tongue as, with the help of the wine, she found herself blowing him a kiss. Then placing herself in God's hands, turned towards the stairs.

Ivan poured himself another drink and rubbed his hands in glee. So, it's not back to mi paltry flat or t'spare room. If that's not t'best Christmas pressie ever, I don't know what is. He drained his glass and climbed the staircase to where his wife lay.

In what had, from day one, been referred to as the marital bedroom. But which Jackie had, hitherto, slept in alone.

# CHAPTER 30

## 26TH DECEMBER 1994
## SEAPORT

'Well. After a day filled wi a bucketful er blessings it didn't end as well as it might've. I'm sorry mi luv.' Ivan reached out to squeeze Jackie's hand. 'I reckon I'd had one too many, after all.'

'Ivan.' Jackie took hold of her husband's hand in return. 'I'll let Candy out, then bring you a cuppa. I reckon now's a good time to begin the real talking. If things are to get better between us. And if you think there's a future for our marriage.'
Ivan hauled himself into a sitting position and rubbed his eyes.

'Aye. Course I do. Be quick though. I'm gasping for a brew.'

Jackie hurried to the kitchen. When she reappeared, she didn't get back into bed but sat on the edge and handed him his Best Dad mug. A present from Laura, filled now with his Yorkshire brew.

Despite her exhaustion and the reassuring sound of Ivan's steady breathing, interspersed with the odd gigantic snore, she'd laid awake most of the night. And, though tempted to creep to the spare room, she'd resisted. But nothing felt right. Fond as she was of her husband; also mindful of the faith they shared, she knew she must be forthright.

'You know I'm deeply fond of you,' she began, taking his free hand.

'Aye, I suppose.' He stared straight ahead.

'And, after all our years together, I can say hand on heart I care tremendously what happens to our marriage. Even the trauma of my discovery brought us closer at first. Don't you think?'

'I know,' he replied at some length, giving his wife's hand another squeeze. 'I've been a so and so.' There was a short pause. 'Always retaliating instead er being forgiving. I'd plenty chance ter mull things over on mi own till I met yon floosie,' he then continued. 'I'm not surprised yer've turned to another woman.'

'No. That's not helpful.' Jackie cut in. 'You're not to blame. Anyway, let's not get bogged down with what the church says. Or what the fundamentalists teach. Not after what we've learned. Through real life experience and getting involved with the Community church. What I'm trying to say is, there's no need for any kind of so-called deliverance. It's what Claudia, despite her Bible based upbringing, has come to realize. And Charles too.'

Ivan jumped right back in.

'I've said umpteen times, I don't know how t'bloke's put up wi it. Not all these years without, yer know. How shall I put it? Without playing away. Goin` off t'rails. He's a better man ner me if he has. But' he went on 'I've grown up. If it's any consolation. I'm not beyond admitting mi behavior can be downright childish. Never heed what I stand for in t'police force.'

Ivan was in full confessional mode. The Holy Spirit had been working in him. Jackie could tell. So decided to seize the moment.

180

'What do you mean?'

'Well.' He began. 'This eye for an eye, tooth for a tooth business. Gets nubdy anywhere. I've learnt t'hard way. Just complicates things.'

You could have heard a pin drop. Until Jackie spoke again.

'You've had an affair.'

She was sitting on the edge of the bed in her fleece dressing gown. She released his hand.

'Aye.' Ivan spoke quietly with none of his usual bluster. 'How do yer know?' His eyes locked with hers for a second, before his gaze fell upon the diamond patterned bedspread.

'Just guessed. And who could blame you? How long did it go on? Is it over?'

Jackie was experiencing pangs of both jealousy and anger. She had always been open with Ivan, however. And felt she had a right to know. She got up to adjust the thermostat, a shiver beginning to creep up and down her spine. While realizing it was a conversation she must see out.

'Oh.' Ivan rubbed his forehead as he did his calculation. 'Must've been three months. Started soon after I left.' He hesitated a second or two. 'But aye. It's over. Finito.' He went on. Flicking away the crumbs from a mince pie, out of a handful he'd secreted upstairs. Lest he should wake in the night.

He turned now to take both her hands in his and to search her face.

'Shall I tell yer summat else?'

'What?' She enquired with trepidation.

'It's time we were dressed.' Jackie was sure feeling the chill. 'Let's make the rest of the day nice for Laura's sake,' she continued, freeing her hand, to go draw back the curtains. 'There's still a covering of the white stuff. Enough, I dare say to take a picture or two before it melts.'

She turned to look at her husband.

'Our daughter's growing up fast. I was hoping for you two to have some fun time together. Although, at least, having you here means she hasn't spent most of Christmas with Ben.'

'Aye. That's a blessing. The lass's far too young for any er that. She needs to get her schooling out er t'way. Anyhow, yer right. We'd best get us skates on. In a manner er speaking. I don't see us shaping` up as t'next Torville and Dean.'

Jackie managed a smile as she climbed into a pair of jeans.

'But before we do,' the inspector went on. 'There's summat else.'

'Oh.' She braced herself.

'Aye. Even before yer met Claudia, I'd been eyeing sumbdy up.' He looked down at the bedclothes again, then at Jackie. 'I've found it hard, not to go looking at other women. It was a weakness. Before I converted to t'faith.' He looked away. 'An` since. If I'm honest.'

'So.' Jackie began. Thinking she'd best let him finish. If the day wasn't to be spent in more agony of heart. Wondering where this had been leading. 'Are you telling me there've been others?' She grabbed a woolly.

'Even before I met Claudia.' She asked. Pulling the jumper over her head.

'There was one.' Ivan replied.

'Oh. Just one. Maybe I should be grateful.'
'Sharon's receptionist,' he went on. Eager to get everything off his chest and get their re-union off on the right foot. 'She's a real un for lettin` it..for leavin nowt`.. for revealin`..'

'Yep. I get the picture.' Jackie interrupted, thinking she'd had all she could take. Until he persisted.

'She invited hersen here. Came about after I let it slip I'd be on mi own. T`weekend yer took Laura to some dance competition or other.'

His wife was now having visions of what had been going on. Long before her and Claudia had even met.

'Any road, nowt happened here.' Ivan had read her thoughts. 'She asked me to her place when I didn't take on, an` was wishin` I'd never opened mi big letter box of a mouth. So, whatever happened an' I'll spare yer t'details, it was only once. Said she was right lonely. Hadn't long been split from her fella.'

Jackie swallowed hard.

'Well, the important thing is we're here together now. And we've talked things through in a civilized manner.' She was about to get up from the edge of the bed when Ivan took both her hands in his.

'One more thing matters though, Mrs. Foster.'

'What's that?' Jackie enquired. There was a gentleness about him she'd not witnessed before.

'Well, from my angle. It'll never occur again. And what didn't happen, here.' Ivan pointed to the middle of the bed. 'What never happened last night, wasn't meant to. If you ask me. I think it's time to draw a line under certain parts of our marriage.'

He gave a wry smile. 'An` just as well. It's not fair. I see that now. You havin` to endure what's no longer a pleasure. I married yer for better or for worse. As yer did me. So, this room's your sleepin` quarters. An` mine'll be over yonder.' He went on, nodding toward the guest room the other side of the landing. 'An` t'other spare can be mi study. Unless yer can suggest summat better.'

Ivan got out of bed and stooped to recover his trousers from the heap he'd left them in.

'There's just one last thing to sort. T'way I see it any road,' he remarked, at receiving no response to his previous comment.

'What's that?' Jackie tentatively enquired as he pulled on the trousers.

'When do you want mi to move back? T'place where I've been shackin' up falls a long way short er luxury. But right enough at only a bob or two rent.'

He'd been renting an apartment in the same block as that of Jodie Chambers. It was how the two had become acquainted. And how one thing had led to another.

'Oh. I didn't know where you'd vanished.' Jackie responded. 'I just had to trust you were OK when you wouldn't tell me. But move in soon as you're packed.' She walked over to him and, looking into his face, touched his cheek.

'Do you know something, Chief Inspector Foster?'

'Go on.' He glanced up from finding the right hole

184

in his new leather belt. A last-minute present from his wife.

'You're my Hero,' She continued now.

And, as she left to prepare breakfast, that glazed look of the previous evening in Ivan's dark eyes, she couldn't help but notice, had been replaced by just a hint of mistiness.

There had been much to come to terms with. But the Fosters had done it, and it was time to move on. For Ivan and Jackie. And for Charles and Claudia Elliott, too.

This life of faith was one heck of a challenge DCI Foster began to reflect. However, of one thing, at least, he was certain. Once having made that commitment there was simply no going back.

He whistled a tune he'd first sung the words to. All of fourteen years ago. At the time of his conversion. As he sat down now with his family, for what had turned into a splendid Boxing Day brunch, the words carried that same weight.

*'I have decided to follow Jesus. I have decided to follow Jesus. No turning back. No turning back.'*

Those words were going round and round in Ivan's head. When filled with so much good grub he could hardly move, his wife handed him another brew.

# CHAPTER 31

'Oh, I'm glad I got you darling. Listen.'

She's won the lottery was Jackie's first thought, knowing how late it was and, despite Claudia not having a gambler's bone in her body.

The two women had enjoyed another wonderful chapter since Ivan's return to the fold. They were just back from a blissful three-night stay in the Cotswolds. So, what could have happened within the short space of time to cause such excitement?

'It's my paintings. I've been in London all day. Then in discussion with Charles.'

Jackie looked at the kitchen clock. It was twenty past ten. She had been doing herself a packed lunch for next day.

'London. What took you to London? Something to do with your paintings.' Jackie was intrigued. Claudia rarely went near the big city after the last series of terrorist attacks. Instead, she would arrive on her spanking new Honda One Two Five.

'Goes faster than the one our old friend Parker-Snellie helped to design,' she'd enthused. 'And it's only a case of the right gear. Whatever our English weather.'

Claudia had given the dream machine her vote of confidence, following its maiden journey to Seaport on Valentine's Day that year. And Jackie had realized she wasn't joking. She'd arrived in record time. Desperate to get the scooter gear off and to affirm their relationship with renewed vigor.

'You remember the batch of oils I did when I was last in Provence,' she went on now.

Jackie recalled the rustic scenes; the lavender fields and the French countryside atmosphere Claudia had captured so vividly.

'Oh, I do.' she replied. 'That wasn't June though, surely. I thought it was long ago.'

'Ah, so you must go. Pity. I haven't finished telling you the story. Time to walk that blest dog, I suppose.'

*'It wasn't only June you produced the paintings. Was it?'* Jackie yelled, taking the phone into the lounge, to avoid waking Ivan who had gone for an early night.

'Ah, no. Most were before that. Only two around Avignon were from June.' Claudia continued. 'I didn't get to show any last year in the end.'

'Oh. I see.' Jackie tried to keep up.

'Anyway, this latest development's sprung from the Stowe exhibition.' Claudia had once been a familiar sight in the tea rooms at Stowe Landscape Gardens, serving refreshments and still had several connections there.

'Oh yes.' Jackie was struggling to keep track. With Claudia darting here and there in her excitement.

'Yes. Jess has been standing in for me. Since I offered her an inducement to do so, until she finds work.'

Claudia's younger daughter's involvement with the art world was more academic than her mother's.

She had recently completed her degree in The History of Modern Art then gone travelling around Europe. On her return, Jess had been happy to fill her time in this way, between job interviews.

Claudia was expert in both oil and watercolors, having spent five years at art school before moving to Parklands. But she lacked the enthusiasm to put her talent on display and the patience to sit still for long periods. And now her daughter's efforts appeared to have paid dividends.

'Jess took a call yesterday while I was out. It was from a Lance de.de...' There was the rustle of paper, followed by, 'here it is. Lance.. Lance de Vallier.'

The agent had spent a good deal of time examining Claudia's work then called his partner and given Jess his card.

'Well, would you believe it?' Claudia continued. 'I phoned him last evening and by lunchtime today, was in his office. He has a couple of studios around our neck of the woods.'

Claudia was referring to the north Cotswolds. An area they adored.

'We must have wandered in scores of times,' she babbled on. 'My friend Daphne's heard of him, too. And if anyone knows who's who in the art world, Daphne does.' There was a silence about long enough for Jackie to digest all this before Claudia was off again.

'He's commissioned me darling.'

'Has he now?' Jackie couldn't help but catch Claudia's excitement. Delighted at the prospect of her success. 'That sounds promising' she went on.

'Yes. He's asked me to paint regularly for him and his French partner, Petula something or other I can't pronounce. Daphne's heard of her, as well.'

'Wow.' Jackie was truly impressed. 'I've always said you could make a living with your talent.'

'You have. But my brain is not wired to cope with business.' Claudia went on. 'Anyway, this charming man, honestly darling you would like him. Lance reckons he has a market for all aspects of my work. Here and abroad. When I showed Charles the.. what do you call them? Oh, you know, *percentages.*' She finally announced and continued in the same animated fashion. 'Well, Lance's secretary had them printed off for me and Charles says it sound like an opportunity too good to miss. And you know how cautious Charles is.'

She paused to take a few sips of water. 'He's offered to oversee the money side, to ensure everything stays legit. And Tristram loves a bit of number crunching. Just like his father. He's sure to get involved if need be.'

Tristram was about to start a postgrad course at the LSE.

'He's got a real head for figures, my son. As well as an eye.' Claudia hesitated and secretly smiled at her own feeble attempt at wit.

'What do you think?' She then asked. Having outlined the facts, keen to get Jackie's reaction.

'What do I think? You must go for it, darling,' Jackie responded. Though, moments later added a word of caution. 'Provided you don't become so busy there's no time for us.'

'Oh, don't worry on that score. And what's more,' Claudia went on. 'I've prayed about it. Not so much.. shall I or shall I not? No, I mean for guidance with the finer detail. All the nitty gritty that goes with me becoming a professional artist and business lady.' Claudia's laugh turned into a chuckle. The idea was, even to herself, amusing.

What was more, Charles Elliott's promise of assistance had been made in the conviction, his wife's latest venture was hardly likely to amount to anything to write home about.

Time, however, was to prove Charles Elliott misguided. But, for the moment, his mere co-operation was quite sufficient to get Claudia's project off the ground. Bringing with it, two women's long held dream of true togetherness, one step closer to fulfillment.

*There's a place for us*
*Somewhere a place for us*
*Peace and quiet and open air*
*Wait for us somewhere.*
*There's a time for us,*
*A time and a place for us*
*Hold my hand and we're halfway there*
*Sometime, somewhere, some day.'*

190

# CHAPTER 32

'There's good news and there's bad. Which do yer want first?'

Ivan was phoning from the Midlands. He'd driven there the previous day handing his caseload to Joe Meredith, his deputy, upon receiving a call from East Midlands General. Gertie Foster was in IT. She'd been involved in what they'd simply referred to as a domestic incident, suggesting Ivan should get there without delay. The Foster couple had helped Ivan's mother's move to a bungalow close to her sister Edie, following their own move south. Edie had recently died, however.

'Oh, I don't mean to sound awful. But can you phone back? I've just got through the door after a nightmare journey and Candy's making a heck of a din..'

'Hey. Steady on. We've all got us problems. Surely I'm entitled to a bit er support from mi missus, in mi moment er crisis. Yer'll wish yer'd listened if I go off t'line. An` before yer say it's time for yer tea, I ain't eaten all day either.'

'Quiet.' She yelled to Candy.

'Go on then love,' she carried on. 'I realize things must be serious for the hospital to call you straight up.' She rarely spoke to him in such terms of endearment. But was experiencing a pang of remorse for her lack of any real show of interest.

'Pity your Pete's abroad.' She went on. 'He's always off the scene when there's trouble.'

Ivan had tried to contact his younger brother before setting out. Single, footloose, and with an eye for the ladies. Especially, 'them of Mediterranean looks with their irresistible charm,' was the way Pete Foster described his unending string of girlfriends.

'Aye. But for once, it's as well he's not 'ere. Or I'd have his abuse to contend wi. On top er everything else. Now, which do yer want first? T'good news, or t'bad.' Ivan repeated his question.

'Alright. I'll have the bad. So long as it's not *too* bad.'

Jackie braced herself. Life had stayed on course for her and Claudia. Her marriage, too, had stabilized beyond anything she could have hoped for, following Ivan's return to the fold.

Please, *please* Lord, she silently pleaded what, to her shame, realized was a prayer of self-interest. Please let nothing have occurred to impact our situation here.

She then remained silent and waited for Ivan to speak again.

'Okey dokey. Well, t'bad news is t'old girl can't go back to t'bungalow. She's conscious an' out er IT. But she'd had a right nasty fall. Been behind t'bedroom door all night.'

Jackie gasped. Unable to find words adequate, she settled for ,'Oh dear.'

'Aye. T'last thing she remembers is feeling dizzy, gettin' ready for bed. Social lot went an' found her yesterday morning when t'cleaner

192

couldn't get in. Jill raised an alert, an` t'neighbor went round wi t'spare key. Found her starkers, they did, nightie strewn on t'floor.'

'Oh, I *am* sorry.' Her weariness paled into insignificance at the scene imprinting itself on Jackie's mind.

'Aye. Knocked hersen clean out before she could activate t'buzzer round her neck.' Ivan went on. 'Any road, I stayed wi her till I'd spoken to t'duty quack.'

'Have you managed to tell your Pete?'

'Not a chance. Still hasn't got himsen a blasted mobile. If he has, he's not letting on. Any road, back to t'good news and why I'm glad lover boy's off t'scene.'

Jackie held her breath as Ivan took his time.

'Wait for it,' he began. Before the length of another silence had her wondering if he, too, had collapsed.

'Ivan. For heaven's sake.'

'Well. No point in letting yer wait any longer, I reckon. Are yer ears pinned back?'

'Right back. As far as they'll go.'

'In that case, here's t'latest from Oz. Great Aunt Flo out in Perth, yer know, yer've met her. We had her to stay a time or two. Remember?'

'Yes. Course. She used to buy a new set of clothes every visit, then tell us to send the lot to Oxfam when she went back.' Jackie recalled.

'Ay well, she'll be needing no more; not even any fancy footwear she liked to trip t'light fantastic in. She's finally popped her clogs.'

'Ivan!'

193

'What?'

'Don't be disrespectful.'

'Aye well. Put more politely, she's been laid to rest at ninety-six and left us a substantial inheritance. Not our Pete. Just me. Well, you an' me. If you play yer cards right, Mrs Foster.' There was a lull while Jackie digested the news and pondered what playing her cards right might entail. Also, she wondered what kind of an inheritance Ivan would consider substantial. He read her thoughts.

'Before yer ask, it's five figures.'

'R..right.' Jackie, even as a woman of faith, was taken aback.

'And how come it's happened right now?' She was skeptical at such sudden good fortune.

'Nay, lass. Yer need ter listen more. An' gab less. Mi mother had been keeping it under her hat for t'last fortnight, hadn't she? Yer knows what she's like, wantin' to keep things equal between me and Pete. She'll be dreading our kid's reaction. If it comes out.'

There followed a considerable silence at Jackie's end.

'Are yer still there?' Ivan finally enquired.

'Yep. Just following instructions.'

'Instructions?'

'You said I was to listen more. And not gab.'

'Aye, well it's nerves kickin' in, wi t'shock. That's what's 'avin' me talk daft instead er being mi usual polite self. Any road, I'm back at t'bungalow, an' just 'avin' a butchers at t'letter.'

'Oh, I see.'

'Aye. T'solicitors in Perth wrote, care of her old address, an` it got passed on. Luckily. Or let's say Sumdy up there was looking after us. Nubdy knew her address. Seeing as we turned down t'invite to t'centenary bash, in eighty-nine.'

Most of the Foster family, including Ivan's great grandfather Jimmy Foster, had sailed to Freemantle on an assisted passage in eighteen eighty-nine. They'd started The Foster Iron and Steel Corporation. It had become a multi-million-pound empire. Ivan's grandfather Leonard was born in a little town called Como but had returned to the UK in his twenties. Ivan's father Frank had been Len and Maggie Foster's only child. Florence Foster, Jimmy's sister, had died a spinster. When Len passed away followed by Frank, Florence had made an amendment to her will, leaving seventy thousand pounds to her favorite nephew Ivan.

'Well, I don't know what to say. I'm a bit gob smacked. That's for sure.' It wasn't an expression Jackie used. Since hooking up with Claudia Elliott, such talk would not normally cross her lips. Five figures though. That, on her reckoning, was somewhere the top side of ten grand. A tidy sum.

'Don't say owt. It's not business to blab about on t'blower. T'last thing I'll say for now is, put a seven in front er four noughts.'

'Seventy thousand.' Jackie converted Ivan's number puzzle into words. Not caring a jot, for once, at his convoluted method of delivering important news. She was amazed.

Furthermore, provided the right solution was found for Gertie Foster's wellbeing, Ivan's good news far outweighed the bad. On a cold and miserable February day across the UK. In the final year of the old millennium.

'Yer've got it lass.' Ivan replied. 'Add a hundred or two for good measure, plus a few bob in interest, by t'time we see it. An' yer've done yer sums right. See yer when everything's sorted up here. Tattie bye.'

# CHAPTER 33

NOVEMBER 1999
PARKLANDS

'Oh marvelous. You're early.

Claudia was beside herself as she beckoned Jackie to sit down for dinner. It was the first Friday in November. Bonfire night, in fact. Jackie took off her leather jacket and pulled up a chair.

'I skipped lunch.' She remarked. Ready to do justice to Claudia's lavish spread. She helped herself to a poppadum while Claudia went to the kitchen. Then, on her return lifted the lids off three piping hot, oven to table ceramic dishes to reveal a sumptuous feast. Consisting of a red meat curry with an exhaustive range of accompaniments.

Jackie began to tuck in.

'This is delicious darling. You've been busy.'

'Not a bit.' Claudia replied. 'All scrambled together easy as pie. If you'll pardon the choice of expression. I cannot imagine how anyone would patronize one of those fast-food establishments springing up all over town.'

Though Claudia's palate was suited to more traditional fayre, she could never do enough to please Jackie, almost ten years into their relationship. She helped herself to a smidgen of rice and a half ladle of curry. Before, right on cue, Jackie provided the opening to steer the conversation toward what was uppermost in Claudia's mind.

'So, what's the latest with your art?'

Claudia reached over to the pine dresser. She took hold of some documents held together by a red plastic spine. She pushed the file across the table.

'You only need look at the first page. Don't concern yourself with the rest.'

Jackie almost choked on a wedge of nan bread which, in her preoccupation with the accounts, had misjudged her gullet could process.

All she'd done was cast a glance over a few rows of figures listed against various titles she recognized as belonging to Claudia's paintings. And there at the bottom of the page were the words: net profit: *twelve thousand seven hundred and thirty-five GBP and twenty-nine pence.* And in figures: *£12,735.29.*

'It's staggering.' Jackie took a slug of water and looked across at Claudia who was beaming.

'Couldn't you have let me in on things sooner? You're a dark horse Claudia Elliott. Even after all these years, there's a side to you I don't know.' She was finding it incredible how such good fortune might have come Claudia's way, out of the blue. As it had for her and Ivan, too.

However, despite the remark, she had not revealed to her details of the Fosters' windfall. Seeing Ivan had stated he'd rather she didn't divulge their business outside the home.

In any case he had only that autumn received the cleared funds. After endless wrangling between two solicitors either side of the world.

'I'm not a dark horse.' Claudia gave a wry smile. 'It's Charles though. He's so cautious. Added to which the first couple of years were nothing to write home about. I said so at the time; just a handful sold here and there plus a few in Holland. Although, I'll admit Lance informed me a while back things were going exceedingly well and would gather pace once my work became known. But Charles said I mustn't get excited too soon'

'Oh.' Jackie put down her cutlery, picked up the file again and examined it in more detail. Then looked over to Claudia still attempting to explain.

'He kept telling me I'd be stung for tax if we'd been given a true representation of things. Anyway, don't let your meal go cold.' Claudia reached out a hand to take the file back. 'Have a closer look later.' She said, placing the file back on the dresser.

'Jolly exciting though. Is it not? Would you like a glass of wine?' Claudia got up, not waiting for an answer, returning two minutes later with, not being much of a drinker herself, a bottle of the tried and trusted Chardonnay. She fetched two glasses.

'Sorry, I forgot in all the excitement.' She remarked, beginning to pour. 'I bought it specially, as well.'

Champagne would be more like it; Jackie could not stop herself thinking but was grateful anyhow. She took a great gulp of the wine and, turning things over in her mind ventured to ask.

'What's the deal with Charles? Is he expecting some share?'

Claudia took a sip of wine.

'What are you getting at? Will Charles want half the proceeds, do you mean?' She put down the glass and looked over at Jackie.

'Yes.' Replied Jackie, savoring her first mouthful of Kiwi Fruit Sorbet oozing with Coconut Sauce. She took a napkin and wiped her chin.

Claudia, meantime, had become defensive towards hubby.

'Why, no. Not at all,' she replied. In any event, Charles had been terribly good to her over the years, and it wouldn't be unreasonable if he did expect to benefit. Not to her mind, anyway. But they were comfortably off, like the Fosters. Therefore, it was no big deal.

Claudia, this time, took a large gulp of the wine before twiddling the stem of her glass, gazing reflectively into it, and realized she was becoming lightheaded. As well as lighthearted again.

'I'm rich, darling. Whoopee.' She exclaimed.

Whipping the napkin off her knee, she got up and flung it in midair, paying no attention to it having landed in a bowl full of chutney.

'So *now,* my precious little lady, before my account's adviser and father of my children gets in from another dull day at the office, you and I have something to celebrate. And there are more exciting ways to do it than stuffing ourselves with food. Come along.'

She grabbed Jackie by the wrists and pulled her up off the chair. 'Let's create a firework display of our own. After which I hope your dinner will have settled enough to manage a slice of my super-sticky parkin. Being the Yorkshire gal that, deep down, I know you forever will be.'

She dragged Jackie, still holding her wrists, to the bottom of the stairs.

'Then, I dare say while you're having your fill of parkin, I'll roast a few chestnuts to round off the evening.'

One hour later, as Charles put his key in the lock, it was, perhaps, by divine arrangement, the cracks and bangs filling the November night air, were long and loud enough, to drown out what was reverberating around the Elliott's upper chambers. In celebration and deep gratitude for all the pair had been so very blessed with.

What Jackie had to decide, as cries of delight gave way to the silent echoes of an especially sweet peace, was how much she should share of her and Ivan's good fortune? With the one who, in all but name, she had come to think of as her life partner.

Also, what exciting possibilities lay ahead for the two of them? Still so in love and now both of considerable means.

It was something they needed to ponder and to pray, earnestly about. As a brand-new millennium came into sharp focus.

Part 4

# CHAPTER 34

30TH JUNE 2000
SEAPORT

Jackie recognized the car parked near their home
when she arrived back from work. It was Friday
teatime. She was shattered and could not, at first,
recall where she'd seen the vehicle before. Then it
dawned. Of course, it was the unmarked police car
D I Stanton, a colleague of Ivan's drove around in.

Graham Stanton sat and watched Jackie take
herself indoors, then went to ring the bell. He had
Adrian Chivers, a uniformed officer, at his side.
Perhaps it *was* Graham who'd been sitting there,
Jackie began to think as, with the chain on, she
peered through the gap. Oh heavens. It was Graham
and a uniformed officer. What could have brought
them? She let them in.

'Shush you.' She yelled to Candy who had
started her usual racket at the sound of the doorbell.
Then she remembered Ivan saying he wouldn't be
needing a meal. He was going to a colleague's
retirement do. It was only quarter past six though,
the celebrations surely wouldn't have started.

Jackie ushered the pair into the lounge once she
had shut the dog out of the way. Still puzzled, she
tried to make light of why the two officers were
there.

'Don't tell me. You've Ivan flaked out in the back of the car before the party's even got going. He never could take his dr..'

Graham cut in.

'No, Jackie love. There's no party tonight.'

She went to put the kettle on, trying to ignore the knotted sensation in the pit of her tummy. As, daring to cast a glance in the officers' direction, she carried on.

'Then what the heck's matter with him? Getting his dates mixed up again. Only last week he had me turn up at the vets for Candy's injection on the wrong day. Don't say he's losing..'

'Nay, Jackie. Sit yerself down.' Chivers, the first northern colleague Ivan had forged ranks with down in Seaport, spoke next. And she could see, as she took her first proper look at him and the other fellow, there was no party spirit behind whatever had brought them to her door. Graham was ashen, as Chivers cleared his throat and, as Jackie flopped onto a dining chair. She stared from one officer to the other. They had followed her through to the kitchen. Maybe they'd simply been in the vicinity and thought they'd join her in a pot of Ivan's favorite Yorkshire brew, before going off duty, Jackie was trying to reassure herself as Chivers spoke again.

'There's been an incident. You need to get down to Castlehampton General. We'll drive you.' He took a deep breath. 'Ivan's been shot.'

'What?'

'Aye. I'm sorry lass. He's in IT.'

'Where? What? Oh, my Good Lord. Help him. Help me.' Jackie got up and staggered toward the hall. 'I'd best see if the phone's working to get hold of Laura. She's just left for the weekend, and it was out of order yesterday. My mobile needs charging, too. Oh, dear, dear God.'

'Nay.' Chivers looked over to D I Stanton before going on. 'Don't fret about t'phone. Let's get you there and find out t'latest. Then contact Laura.'

Graham put an arm round Jackie's shoulder.

'Adrian's right, love. Collect what you need. We'll fill you in with what we know on the way. Might not turn out as bad as it sounds.'

'Oh, my Good Lord. I hope not. This is awful. What about Candy?'

The hound was howling again. She needed feeding and walking.

Graham got his mobile out. 'Friend? Neighbor? Is there someone we can call?' Jackie gave him the number of a neighbor who they worshiped with at the Lantern. Brenda lived in the next road. She had a key and came to exercise Candy now and then.

Jackie emerged from the downstairs bathroom just as Graham got through to Brenda.

'Ask her to get the Lantern to pray,' she pleaded. Graham handed her the phone. Jackie took it and began to share what she could. Bren said course she would set up a prayer chain and come right away.

Chivers was standing next to the kettle alongside the tea mugs Jackie had got out. He held up one and looked her way, thinking a sweet drink would help. Jackie shook her head.

'No. Let's go.'

At five to seven the three arrived at reception. They were directed straight to IT.

'Mrs. Foster?' A kindly nurse led Jackie down a corridor.

On the way there, she had learned Ivan and another plain clothes officer had been following a murder suspect heading for Seaport Harbor. With just minutes to spare before the suspect reached the port, the officers had rammed his vehicle. The suspect had jumped out and fired three pistol shots. The first one had missed both men. The second had skimmed the other officer's head as he dived for cover. But Ivan had taken a direct hit. He'd been half conscious on the ground in a pool of blood, by the time the emergency services got there. Chivers and several armed officers had raced to the scene and disarmed the suspect. Graham had turned up as the ambulance sped off. Lights flashing and sirens blaring.

Stanton paced up and down in the hospital corridor now, awaiting the moment Ivan regained consciousness. What so and so had done this to their colleague and friend?

No worse, physically, for his part in the drama, Chivers went in search of coffee. He tapped out a text on his mobile then hit the send to all button.

The retiring officer's party was cancelled, till the situation with DCI Foster became clear.

At seven twenty-eight by the waiting area clock, Jackie reappeared, a white coated medic at her side. Ivan's wife's face was the color of the doc's coat. The expression on both of their faces said it all.

Jackie walked toward the two officers, then turned and broke into a run, hurtling into the nearest lavatories which happened to be the Gents. She whizzed past a startled elderly man, slammed the door of a cubicle, and threw up. Retching over and over. Long after every morsel of the paltry amount she'd eaten that day had been ejected from her gut. The nurse who'd greeted her on arrival came to check she was OK when, shaking, she emerged from the washrooms.

Meanwhile, the doctor had taken the officers aside, detailing how the bullet had passed through the left ventricle of Ivan's heart. He had been fortunate to survive the ambulance journey, in view of the blood loss, he explained. Then, despite all attempts to save him, Ivan had died shortly before their arrival.

So, in a matter of hours, it had turned, quite literally, into the first bloody summer of the millennium. Of a kind no-one would have wanted to predict.

D I Stanton and Chivers choked back tears, as Chivers sent an update to friends and colleagues, before the press went to town.

Jackie took hold of Graham's mobile and summoned the courage to call their daughter.

Laura Jane Foster was having supper with her boyfriend. And at twenty years of age, was about to receive devastating news.

# CHAPTER 35

## 1ST JULY 2000
## PARKLANDS

It was three in the morning when Claudia heard the phone go. She'd awoke and got up to make herself one of the endless cups of Earl Grey that got her through many a broken night. There was something different about this wee small hour awakening though.

She had been roused from an unusually deep sleep then gone with her cuppa, to lift the Bible, kept next to her prayer chair. The Bible had fallen open at *Psalm 23*. She'd begun reading and reached 'Yea, though I walk through the valley of the shadow of death' when the phone started ringing. She would have gone to wake Charles, on account of her apprehension. Who could it be at that hour? Her instinct, however, told her not to fetch Charles. She picked up the phone.

'Hello.'

There was no sound which she could make out. She tried again.

'Hello, Kentley three three six nine three. Who is this please?'

Still nothing. Then, even without her device, deep racking sobs could be heard. Accompanied by a young female voice.

'It's Laura. My mum can't speak. She's too upset.' More sobbing ensued. Plain enough for Claudia to recognize as coming from Jackie.

'Oh, my goodness, Laura. What's the matter?'

'It's dad. I've just got here, and mum asked me to phone.'

There was a muffled sound. Then further sobbing. And a high-pitched wailing noise which Claudia thought must be coming from the dog. Seeing Jackie had spoken of a need to possibly have her put down, due to age-related issues. Although Laura had said it was something to do with her father. And they wouldn't call in the middle of the night over some crisis with that wretched animal. Surely. But it was Laura who'd lost control of her emotions, before managing to stammer, 'M-mum's here.' Jackie took the phone.

Claudia's heart was pumping fast. She went back to her chair with the phone. Her legs were giving way.

'Darling what on earth..?'

'It's Ivan. He's gone.'

Claudia groaned.

'Oh, no. Not again. You mean he's gone off in the middle of the..'

'No. He-he's been shot. He's gone. I need you. Can you come?'

'Well, yes. But how do you mean...gone? Oh Lord. You're not ...darling, you're not telling me, you're not saying Ivan's died.'

'Look. I'm telling you. I got back from the hospital several hours ago. He'd been shot. There was an incident. Oh God. If only I could have been there sooner. I never got to say goodbye.'

More sobbing and wailing could be heard.

Then again. 'Please darling. I beg you. Do come?'

The next few hours were a blur.

Charles became aware something was afoot, just as Claudia had decided she'd better wake him. He'd donned his dressing gown and entered the kitchen to find his wife getting into her scooter gear. Her machine out of the shed, at the ready.

'What the dickens is going on? It's not even daylight. What are you up to?'

It was Saturday and they'd arranged a trip to her most esteemed furniture outlet. Some item, a real must have, she'd told him, was going to be drastically reduced.

'You're not going into town to be first in the queue for whatever it is you've had your eye on. Not at this hour. For pity's sake. I thought we were both going when the place opens.'

As Charles stood in the middle of the kitchen, however, he realized he was missing the mark by a mile. She'd hardly noticed he was there and hadn't heard a word. She reached for some tissues and blew her nose. He could see she'd been crying. She looked over to him.

'Oh, Charles. It's the most appalling news. I was about to wake you. I must get down to Seaport. Ivan's been shot while on duty.'

'Wh-what? Oh, dear God.' Charles rubbed his eyes and gave his head a shake in an effort to come to. What, where... where *is* Jackie? At the hospital, I guess.'

'No. Alas, too late by the time she got there. It was fatal. Gunshot wound to the heart.'

Charles put a hand on the worktop to steady himself.

'Oh no.'

Claudia went and touched him on the shoulder. She gazed into his chalk white face.

'Oh, Chas, I hope you don't mind. Jackie needs me. I must go.'

'Why yes. Of course. But for heaven's sake let me run you. Has anyone told Laura? Poor girl.'

'Yes. She's with Jackie.'

Charles straightened up.

'Well, give me half an hour and I'll take you. Stay long as need be.'

Claudia took hold of him in a bear hug. Then, still clad in her gear, she pulled away.

'That's jolly decent of you, Chas. You truly are my rock. Will you be alright though?' She tried to think clearly. 'There's not a lot in the freezer precooked. Oh, dear God. Poor Jackie.'

Claudia was torn at a whole new level.

'Don't worry on my account. I was going to tell you, I'm over in Brussels for a few days the end of next week.' Charles was still groggy. But his mind began racing.

Claudia was taking her scooter pants off. With one leg in and one out, she halted and looked in his direction.

'Again? Are you sure they're not lining you up for a transfer? It's becoming far too frequent.'

'No, no, no. Just more wretched meetings with Eurostar's big shots. Timetable co-ordination, or something needing intense scrutiny. Just an excuse for a few four course dinners in five-star luxury's more like it. I'll not be going short of a square meal or two. So don't worry.'

210

Charles turned on his heel.

'Anyway, I'd better get dressed.' The light was starting to filter through the kitchen blind.

'Get yourself some things packed, if you haven't done, then we'll be off, before the weekend traffic starts. Have you eaten at all?'

'No. Can't face a thing.'

'Me neither. I could do with a pot of strong tea though.'

'Yes.' Claudia replied and went to refill the kettle.

Charles headed for the stairs.

'Oh, my Lord. Whatever next?' He mumbled on his way up.

The journey down in Charles's Ford Mondeo was completed in silence. Except for Claudia's intermittent sobbing. Charles was a good driver. The car, if not the last word in luxury, was comfy. And with hardly any traffic, Charles was lost in his thoughts as they travelled along, as Claudia became lost in hers. By the time they reached Seaport, it had been speedy, safe and, at the very least, civilized.

Charles helped Claudia out with her things then said goodbye. He couldn't cope with three distraught women and whoever else might be there, if he ventured inside. He wasn't good at that kind of thing. He checked his watch.

God willing, he'd be back at Parklands long before lunchtime. Which would suit him very well.

# CHAPTER 36

By mid-morning Jackie was sobbing her heart out in Claudia's arms, in the privacy of her bedroom. Laura was hanging on to Candy who kept emitting a gruesome howl, aware something was up.

Life could never be the same. But the Foster family would soldier on. All pulling together as never before, including Laura's uncle Pete whom they had just managed to inform. What and the rest of them were facing, would hopefully make him grow up.

Gertie Foster had been taken into care. Having developed severe dementia soon after her fall. It may have been one of those blessings which come in a heavy disguise. Gertie had always secretly idolized her elder son. Now, Pete Foster had the unenviable task of trying to break the sad news to his mother. It wouldn't be easy. She hadn't recognized either him or Ivan since being admitted to the nursing home.

As for Laura, she had wanted to get engaged, although her parents had been against it. Seeing she had just started vet's college, to train for the career she'd set her heart on. Until she had fallen head over heels for an older man, a lecturer at the college. On the positive side, Guy Andrews was from a Christian background. So, it was hoped he would now turn out to be everything Laura needed, to get her through this dreadful time. A premarital test. With or without any engagement.

And Jackie had Claudia. What a blessing that was. She would never have got by without her.

Meanwhile, back at Parklands Charles was putting an international call through to a little town in Belgium.

'Charles. Oh, my Charles. How vonderful to hear you. And vat a surprise! Ees vifie avay for veekend?'

'Yes. And nice to speak to you too, my lovely. Wifie's away for a while.'

'Reelly. Provence?'

'Yes. Really. But no, she's not in Provence, my sweet. It's taken a real tragedy to free me up this time. Sadly.'

'Oh, non, non. Tragedee not good.'

'No. Indeed. But listen. Give me chance to study the train times and I plan to be with you. It'll be midday tomorrow before I get there, I expect. Unless I decide to drive through the night. Anyway, glad I caught you, my precious. I'll go now to work out the logistics.'

'Logeestics? Ees dat someting concerning tragedee? Eet's not your familee, ees eet? Oh, Charles, I hop not.'

'No. Bless you. The family's fine. I simply mean I need to get on with my travel arrangements. Then I'll explain. You're free Sunday, I trust. And how are you placed for the next few days? I'm trying to wangle the whole week off.'

Charles tapped the train timetable sitting on the shelf next to the phone, with the end of a ballpoint pen in his free hand, lost in thought.

'Can be done.' He then continued. 'In view of my senior role.'

213

Vangle, Charles. Vat ees vangle? You must teach me dat word. Eet does sound eenteresting, and a beet rude. Olso... yoor senor role? Ooh, that reely turns me on. Ees eet Spaneesh?'

'What?' Charles scratched the top of his head. 'Wangle. Oh, I mean try to arrange some unplanned leave. And *senior* role is my ranking with the railways. Nothing to do with Spain.'

He creased his brow. Blimey Charles, you know how to pick 'em ran through his frazzled mind. First a wife who's as deaf as a post. Then a mistress who speaks hardly any English.

'I'll check in somewhere for a night when I first arrive if you like. Since I'm coming at such short notice,' he remarked, returning to practicalities.

'Oh, non. You veel not, monsieur. There veel be dinner and champagne avaiting you, at your arrival. And then some... er, vat do you eenglish call it? Some, maybe, some saucee reading. To put you in the right mood for our re-oonion. Ooh la la and bon voyage, mon ami. A bientot.'

'Yes, absolutely. Then, once I've digested some rather shattering news, of no concern to your pretty little head and with madame's comforting arms round about me, I'm sure I shall need nothing else. See you my love in just a few hours.'

Charles rang off and with pen at the ready, hurried to his study to fill in a form headed *Senior Management Emergency Leave*.

Celine LaMonte, too, put down the receiver and rifled through her wardrobe till lighting upon her most alluring outfit. Before settling down, full of joyful anticipation. For what would have been an interminably long wait.

Had it not been for a tray of very fine truffles, along with a large bottle of Ginderella. Placed conveniently by the side of her bed.

# CHAPTER 37

'Oh, if you could have been at the funeral, Chas. All those officers carrying the coffin. They almost outnumbered the relatives.'

'Yes. Well, I told you. I'm busy with work. They're constantly calling me over to Brussels.' Charles picked up the weekend Telegraph which had just arrived. He made a show of reading the paper, continuing to speak from behind it. 'Anyhow, you were there to support Jackie. It would have been awkward with me by your side.'

'I know.' Claudia replied, pushing the bowl of blueberry yoghurt away, to join a half-eaten croissant. At least she was losing weight, regardless of not having done a stroke of swimming or any cycling since the drama unfolded.

'I just wish you'd been there when I tried to phone. Especially the week Ivan died. It was so hard on Jackie. Also, I wasn't sure where I slotted in. Once the relatives arrived.'

'I told you I was in Brussels.'

'Yes. I tried the number you gave me several times.'

'I never received any calls. Telecommunications have a long way to go over there.'

Claudia got up to dispense herself a coffee from the new machine she'd picked up while shopping in Castlehampton, before getting the train home.

'You could have phoned the minute you got back. Would you like coffee?'

Charles put the paper down.

'No thank you. You know I like tea in the morning. Look Claudie. We need to have a natter. Let me know when you've recovered enough from what I realize has been a traumatic time. Then we'll chat.'

'Cat. Did you mention some cat? You know I can't stand them. If it's that stray, filthying my flower beds again, I'll..'

'*Chat*, Claudie. Chat.' Charles got up. 'Where's the blessed device? Go get it. Then we need to talk.'

'I can't. It's in Seaport where I left it.'

She'd got on the wrong train and had to re-route from Bristol with the help of a fellow passenger, having misheard the announcements. But wasn't about to admit that.

'Alright, you haven't got your device. Well then, let you and I get up a tad closer and more personal than we have been accustomed to in recent years.' Claudia handed Charles the tea. He took it and sat down before beckoning his wife to pull up a chair. He clasped her right hand in both of his.

'Look. I know you've had a lot to deal with.'

'You can say that again,' she remarked. 'Although it's Jackie and Laura I'm thinking of. At least I've still got you.'

Charles took the plunge.

'You have and you haven't. The new millennium's about to spring more surprises.'

'What *do* you mean?' Claudia turned red in the face. She pulled her hand free and got up. 'I can't

217

take any more, Charles. Oh, Good Lord. I told you to get that funny lump checked out. I'll get you an appointment first thing Mond..'

'Wait. It's not my health. I didn't say any *nasty* surprises. The lump's gone. I told you it was nothing. Just a cyst.'

'Well, that's a relief.'

'Yes. It's the job though.' Charles cleared his throat. 'I'm afraid I was less than honest with you. While you were in the throes of distress over Jackie, the morning I ran you down there.'

Something clicked. Deep down in Claudia's soul. She flopped back onto the chair and sat motionless, trying to read Charles's face.

'So, you *are* getting a transfer to Brussels. I was right.'

Charles caught her eye.

'Yes. I'll be chief liaison officer between Eurostar and British Rail. At nearly twice my current salary. Good job I kept brushing up on my French, the few times I've accompanied you to Provence.'

Charles had been in line for the position for a while, following an interview in the spring. Whereupon his arrival home from the visit to Celine, there had been a letter giving him a start date. It was the moment he realized he couldn't withhold the news any longer.

'Good job for *who*?' Claudia got up again and burst into tears. 'Oh Chas, I just said. I can't take it.' As her intuition came right to the fore, she continued her rant. 'It's not just the job. Is it?' A deep sob escaped her. 'I'm sure your French will be a real asset for you and whoever you're in cahoots with, over there.'

She flung a tea towel picked up to dab her eyes on, across the kitchen. It landed on the gas hob, close to a ring burning merrily away since breakfast. 'And I couldn't care less about the salary increase. I've got my paintings to fall back on. Haven't I?'

Charles became silent. He went to make himself another brew. Rescuing the tea towel on his way, he switched off the ring. Always mindful of the bills he would do a quick check each time he entered a room. That morning he had not. His thoughts being elsewhere.

Claudia thumped the table with her fist. 'Damn. Oh! Bloody well *damn*.'

Charles kept his composure and spoke in almost a whisper. Words not intended for anyone, particular. He just needed to express them.

'It had been coming. For a long, long time. It had surely been coming.'

Claudia ran from the kitchen, up the stairs. She slammed the bedroom door and in her hour of great need, could not even bring herself to phone Jackie.

And as she cried out to God in anguish, she was far from sure, whether she wanted to see Jackie Foster. *Ever*, if ever again.

# CHAPTER 38

## 5TH AUGUST 2000
## SEAPORT

'Laura. Have I missed any calls from Claudia?' Jackie had been laid low by her prescribed sedation in the days following Ivan's funeral. But she was off the pills and back at work, after a month's compassionate leave. Laura was home till September. Jackie had been glad of her company and that of Guy, to look after the place and Candy, too. There had been no word from Claudia for over a fortnight though. Regardless of being without her device and Jackie having left a voicemail to remind her.

'No mum. There's been no word from Claudia.' Laura replied.

Despite being utterly drained by the end of week one back at work and devoid of any real emotion, Jackie decided she'd best give Claudia a ring. If only to try and re-establish some sense of normality. Lifting the handset, she was confident she had hit the right button. And yes, there was an answer.

'Hello darling. How are you? Did you get my message?' Jackie launched in upon hearing a female voice. Then thought Claudia sounded strange. Perhaps she had dialed the wrong number. But that was not the case.

'If you mean Claudia, she's not here. I'm her sister. Who is this, please?'

'Oh. No worries. I'll phone again.' Jackie was taken aback but not of the mind to go into explanations with strangers. It was odd though. Claudia had barely mentioned she had a sister.

'I'm afraid you won't get her.' The unfamiliar voice went on. 'I'm house-sitting while she's away.'

'Away? Ah, I didn't realize but I have her mobile number. Good evening.'

'You won't get her on that. It'll be switched off.' Marguerite Wilson caught Jackie as she was about to ring off. Her curiosity aroused, as to whose darling Claudia might be. Also, whether it could have any bearing on the problems her sister was currently facing and the reason for Charles's frequent absence. Marge, as she was known, wasn't troubled, whatever the case. She had experienced little in the way of the benefits her older sister enjoyed and appeared to take for granted. So, a brief spell living in luxury at the Elliott's expense was never going to be questioned.

Jackie, at needing to put an end to the conversation replied, 'Well, thank you.' Then quickly hung up.

What was going on at Parklands? Where was Charles? Brussels, Jackie supposed. He spent an awful lot of time there. She got out her mobile, thinking she should have tried her that way in the first place. The precious little Nokia 3210's had been a Godsend. Ever since they'd sprung onto the market. She scrolled through to Claudia's number, pressed the call button then waited for the ringtone. Instead, she got a voice almost as familiar to her as Claudia's. And exactly as Marge had predicted.

*'Welcome to the Orange answer phone. The person you are calling is not available. Please leave a message after the tone.'*

Their relationship had survived on those messages when all else failed. Now Claudia wasn't even returning hers. Well, it *was* half past nine. She could be in company. Although that wasn't such a good prospect without her device, Jackie reflected. Either for Claudia, or the company she might be keeping. She was more likely to have gone to bed, wherever she was, she decided. Still puzzled, she dare not entertain any of the sinister thoughts making a bid to fill the vacant space in her head. She left another message.

'Darling. Can you call me soon as you get this? I'm back at work and I need to know you're alright. Also, I've got your hearing thing. Love you and miss you. Kiss kiss kiss.'

That had been Friday night. Saturday came and went with no word. Jackie had been beside herself. It was a worry she could have done without, as her buried emotions began to resurface. They had parted so lovingly, too. In view of the awful circumstances.

Well, she'd have one more go at the home phone after lunch next day. Claudia would be in church somewhere, Sunday morning, Jackie guessed. Then the thought occurred she ought to get herself to the Lantern. It was where she had received most support since being widowed. The Community church were sympathetic, of course. But they had never understood why she and Claudia hadn't got together, 'properly' as they saw it, long ago. When the love they shared was so plain to see.

Well, now that love was being tested and the dynamics had changed. Four had become three. Was it time to face the fact their long-term romance had been nothing more? An extra marital affair which had run its course and burnt itself out. At the worst possible time for Jackie. Had Claudia got cold feet in Jackie's hour of need?

The next seven days were destined to tell. For the moment, however, her heart was filled with a kind of grief and an anxiety even her faith could barely sustain. As she set her face for another week at Winwood Crown Court. How much longer she could endure that situation, she did not know.

'One day at a time Sweet Jesus' was playing on her radio that Sunday night when, still without a single word from her loved one, she got ready for bed. As she turned back the covers, she joined in the last line of the song.

*'Lord for Thy sake, please help me to take*
*One Day at a Time.'*

# CHAPTER 39

SATURDAY 12<sup>TH</sup> AUGUST 2000
SEAPORT

'Letter for you mum.' Laura yelled to Jackie, as she picked up their post on her way out with Candy. She put the item on the phone shelf.

Those words had a familiar ring. From the recesses of her mind Jackie recalled that same scenario one Saturday morning. All of ten years ago when Laura was only a girl. Exactly as she had then, Jackie hurried from kitchen to hall. And yes, there it was. An envelope bearing now unmistakable writing and containing a notecard.

`Darling...thanks for the messages and the letter. Please ring. I'll be home by noon Saturday. Lots to tell. Xxx`

Jackie had posted a final note following the unanswered voicemails, offering up a prayer for some reply. She thanked The Good Lord for His answer, but could not wait for midday, trying every five minutes from eleven thirty. Until she got the woman who she realized, even in her state of trauma, meant the world to her, on the line.

'Hello. Is it Mr. Stribley? I expect you're ringing to say I left my specs.'

'Mr. Stribley? Noo. It's your one and only true love, I still dare to presume. Unless that's why I've not heard anything. Have I been replaced? Who's Mr. Stribley? And what, may I ask, might you have been taking off for him besides your specs? No wonder I couldn't get you.'

Jackie managed a bit of light banter, despite her grief-stricken heart.

'You asked me to phone,' she continued.

Claudia, it seemed, was now without hearing device and specs, too.

'Oh darling, it's you. Yes, I did say phone. How's things? Sorry to have put you through this. On top of everything else. Is Laura home?'

'Yes. Thank God. And Guy's here some of the time. Good job too. Where the hel... where the heck have you been?' Jackie's relief was turning to anger. Surely Claudia could have stayed in touch.

'Oh, Nigel Stribley is one of those - you know, one of those legal bods, sol...solicitors,' she stammered. 'I've just got back.'

'Solicitors?' Jackie was mystified. 'But they don't open Saturdays. Not down here, anyway,' she went on. 'And if you mean you've been at the solicitor's all this time, you'll have to mortgage Parklands to pay the bill.'

Claudia had never visited a solicitor. In all the time they'd been together. Not as far as Jackie knew.

'Is there an issue with your paintings?'

Claudia wasn't making sense.

'Paintings? No, that's the least of my worries. Provided Lance keeps notching up the sales. And so long as I keep churning the work out.'

Claudia gave a carefree laugh. Then became more serious.

'No. It's Charles and me. We're getting a divorce. That's why you've heard nothing. I've

225

been away for three whole weeks while he moved out.'

'Whaat?' Jackie couldn't take it in. They say it never rains but it pours. It was the last thing she considered welcome news. So soon after her own devastating loss.

Claudia gave an intake of breath.

'It is so. I hadn't been back from yours long when things blew up.'

'Well. I don't know what to say.'

'No.' Claudia responded sheepishly. 'I should have told you. I guess. But I needed time to think. Took myself down to Dorset.'

'Dorset? All that way' Jackie continued with raised voice, beginning to wonder whether her own hearing was not all it should be.

'Yes.'

'But not on your scooter?' Jackie was totally perplexed. She hadn't gone all that way using that mode of transport without her device. Surely.

'Yes, course. It's not much further than coming to yours. I'd a couple of weeks around Hardy Country. Did me a power of good. We must go there sometime.'

Well, at least they were still an item after Claudia's soul searching. The next question was whether to probe further. Or let Claudia tell the whole tale when good and ready. She could not visualize though, the moments of chaos for Claudia and even more so, for those she had met on her travels, minus the device. She was still pondering this as Claudia continued.

'My sister came to stay once Charles had moved out. I didn't tell her he'd left, seeing we've never been close, because of that awful husband of hers. Long distance lorry driver. Even been prosecuted for drink driving. Broke my parents' heart, it did, when he got her pregnant at seventeen. Anyhow, I told Marge I was going to stay at a health farm. And with Charles away, too, wondered if she'd care to look on to give herself a nice break. Some of Charles's things are still here; so it was plausible.'

Jackie didn't let on she'd spoken to Marge. Though did venture to ask.

'Where's Charles gone?'

'Belgium.'

'Ah.'

'Yes. Need I say more?'

Jackie had expressed surprise on several occasions, at how much time Charles spent there.

'Got a transfer to Brussels.' Claudia went on. 'Lias.. liaison something or other high up connected to Eurostar.'

'Oh, I see.'

'Yes. And shall I tell you something else?'

'Go on.'

'I don't give a damn.' Claudia's voice took on a lighter note again.

'You don't?' Jackie was more than a little surprised.

'No.' Claudia went on. 'I spent some time at a Christian retreat whilst down *theyur in deeperst Dourset.*' She did a good imitation of the accent providing evidence she'd somehow been in communicado with the locals.

'You did.'

'Yes. And this is the conclusion I've reached.' Claudia paused, before going on.

'As Christians, divorce is never ideal, but neither is your becoming widowed so young. God's ways are not ours. And the timing of all this has convinced me you and I are meant to be together.'

The tears trickling down Jackie's cheeks were a mixture of relief, gratitude and sorrow.

'Oh, darling. Say no more. I've never been so glad to hear that. All I need now is to be in your arms.'

Claudia's heart melted at the thought of her lover's arms round about her.

'Oh, I know. It's such a healing. Especially in times such as this. Shall it be yours, or mine? And when?'

'Yours. And better be the weekend now I'm back at work.'

Jackie could not envisage getting through the week but could see the logic. 'It makes sense,' she remarked and Claudia agreed, adding, 'Meantime, I need to find my spare specs. Or pay the dashing Mr. Stribley one more visit.'

'Hey, hold on. Otherwise, you'll find me up there sooner. I can see I must keep a close eye on things. Also, you need to get that earpiece which I'll be bringing, in place. So, I can issue instructions on how not to behave with dashing solicitors. And before I'm tempted to use every bit of legal clout at my disposal to find an excuse to get him struck off.'

'Pardon darling. I haven't heard a word. I think there's something matter with your phone.'

At this Jackie replaced the receiver and began to prepare herself for that oh so familiar trip.

A trip that would soothe and, God willing, would heal. To pave the way for all kinds of possibilities. With the passage of a little more time.

# CHAPTER 40

There had been no seasonal festivities at number One Blenheim Drive. Once the two women became reunited, the year for Jackie had passed in a daze as she drove to and from work. Simply going through the motions with her job. Then taking herself up to Parklands most weekends. Or entertaining Claudia, on those occasions she made it down to her.

The reality, for the Foster widow, once it hit home, was somber. There was deep sorrow life had dealt her such a blow. Especially when she saw Laura blossoming into the kind of woman any father would be proud to call his daughter. And Guy's tenderness, his encouragement spurring her on to complete the qualification she had worked her socks off to achieve. This had upset Jackie most in the autumn when the couple did get engaged. With no Ivan to share the celebration. Laura and Guy were meant for each other. The unfolding of events had made clear. How blessed her pa would have been if he had lived to see it all. In moments like these Jackie hid her grief even from Claudia, who had her loss to fully come to terms with.

Therefore it was too soon to make plans. They both first needed closure.

Jackie had spent the whole of Christmas Day in tears. Whenever left alone. Having gone over and over in her mind Ivan's return home, following their months apart. It was less than six years ago. If her husband did have to die, how differently she might have processed things. If, in those final days, she'd been wholeheartedly committed to the marriage. She hid these regrets from Claudia. Along with the question, was God punishing her for this?

Emphatically no, being the conclusion Jackie had reached after placing herself in the hands of a professional counsellor, a lady from outside the church. And why would God want to punish Laura? Beth Mellor had pointed out. Things happened and policing was becoming more dangerous every day. Once such issues were resolved, the way would, hopefully, become clear for a new chapter in the women's lives to unfold. With Claudia's husband, too, off the scene.

Charles had taken on a new lease of life upon securing the affections of a lady ten years his junior. He'd been delighted to place an engagement ring on Celine's finger. After which there was no hurry. Especially with no question of children. Ms LaMonte having suffered a miscarriage in her thirties which had left her infertile. Being not of the maternal kind when the pregnancy occurred, Celine had put it all down to a twist of fate. Which had caused her, nevertheless, to search for the true meaning of life.

Following her quest, she had embraced the Christian faith at a level matching that of her new fiancé. Not all consuming. But sufficient to convict her to say her prayers every night. For guidance in situations of uncertainty and comfort in times of trouble. Also, to attend church on occasions, meaning there were no issues on that score to resolve. Indeed, the couple were in total agreement, it was none other than the Hand of The Almighty Who had been their matchmaker.

Notwithstanding all this, a certain discretion was still needed within the Elliott family.. The girls had been fine when faced with their mother's lifestyle since their parents' divorce. Carolyn continued to live in the States, loosely following the faith she was brought up in. She had been engaged for several years to stockbroker, Brad. As for Jess, she had always been closer to her mother than the rest. Finding daddy, a little more aloof than she would have liked. Besides, she was more open minded than her siblings and had departed from her traditional upbringing and on the point of exploring her own sexuality. It was Tristram though. He, too, had left the church and its teachings. But he idolized Charles and found his mother's artistic temperament difficult to accommodate. However, like his sisters, Tristram was brought up to not always be forthright in airing his views or giving vent to his feelings. He had made a point of taking himself away from home when Jackie was around. If Tristram had inherited any trait from his mother, it was her snobbery. He was disapproving of Jackie's north country accent which, though no longer pronounced, was beyond disguise. So, if mama couldn't live happily without these intruders upon the scene, then, thought Tristram, she should be more circumspect concerning those with whom she chose to take her amusement. He had been cool on the phone, the few times they'd spoken, since his father left. Then had arranged a ski trip to the Swiss Alps, taking in the whole of Christmas and New Year.

Carolyn had made a brief trip from the States with Brad to visit her mother at the start of the break, followed by a plane hop to Brussels. Upon their return to the UK, Carolyn had managed to raise Claudia's spirits with the surprise news of the couple's forthcoming marriage plans next Spring.

When Jackie heard, she began to live in hopes she and Claudia would attend as a couple. And that once Christmas two thousand was behind them, things would, in every way, begin to look up.

It was to be her mantra for the New Year. When, as Big Ben chimed midnight, and with Claudia's arms round about her, they shared their first two thousand and one kiss.

# CHAPTER 41

MONDAY 1st SEPTEMBER 2003
THE COTSWOLDS

Rupert Brookes glanced up from his work to catch
sight, through a side window, of a middle-aged
woman propping a scooter on its stand. His first
thought was she had to be local. Considering the
mode of transport at only ten past nine on a Monday
morning looking a lot like rain.

Claudia took off her helmet and tucked it under
her arm before stepping inside the office of Rumsey
and Routledge, one of the UK's leading property
agents.

This was surreal; Brookes began to think. Their
first client of the week could have landed from
another planet.

'Good morning Madam. Can I help you?' He
enquired.

'I beg your pardon. What say you?' Claudia
responded a little too loudly, looking the astonished
fellow in the eye. As he got to his feet Brookes cast
a glance towards his colleague. Her attention having
been averted from a computer screen, to satisfy her
curiosity as to who or what, had come through the
door to bring a touch of mirth to the life of R and
R's north Cotswold branch on a dull and overcast
Monday morning.

Brookes walked round to the front of his desk.
He raised his voice to what he hoped was a more
suitable pitch.

'Can I help you, madam? Is there something you have in mind?'

'Oh yes, I'll say. Otherwise, I wouldn't be here. Now would I?'

Still bemused, Brookes stood and looked expectantly over to where Claudia was flattening out a paper bearing details of a property around Chipping Norton.

'It's this.' Claudia pointed to a dwelling she had circled in red pen. 'It looks delightful I must say. Still available, I take it?' She removed her gaze from the paper and fixed it back on the agent who was hurrying over to where she appeared to have taken root. He had a peep.

'Oh, Artists Cottage. It certainly is. Not for long though, I shouldn't think.' He went to the filing cabinet then handed his client the particulars. 'Here we are. Only came on two weeks ago. But there's been lots of interest.'

After examining each of the photographs, Claudia began to read out, in a voice normally reserved for one of her ladies' afternoon tea speeches: 'Quintessential Cotswold Cottage. *Exquisite* Landscaped Gardens. Open Plan Sitting Room and Kitchen. Inglenook Fireplace. Three Bedrooms. Family Bathroom and Downstairs Cloakroom. This superb property is available for offers in the region of one hundred and seventy-five thousand pounds.'

'I *can* read, madam.' The agent had muttered through closed teeth while glancing at the floor, then again at his colleague whose head had disappeared beneath the desk, her shoulders shaking as she retrieved a file.

Claudia folded the leaflet and removed her metal rimmed specs.

Brookes took a deep breath. He'd only been in the business a year, and this was his most curious client, to date.

'Would you like details of anything else Madam? Are you local? Do you have anything to sell? Can we arrange you a viewing?'

'No, no, and two maybes. Thank you kindly. And *good* day.' Claudia had tucked the leaflet inside the paper she'd brought along, marched from the office and deposited the lot in her scooter box.

It was starting to drizzle as, off she sped, back towards Kentley Manor. A bit of rain wasn't going to dampen her spirits. Or her bright idea. Oh no!

The time had come to put not only her prized machine into gear. But her well-honed powers of persuasion, too. And sooner, she had decided, by the time she reached Parklands. Rather than later.

# CHAPTER 42

Jackie was nodding in her chair after a hectic day.
The phone startled her. She staggered up to go
answer it.

'Seaport five one four two eight.'

The line was charged with excitement. And there
was only one on her Caller Accept list who could
have something to get excited about on a soaking
wet Monday evening.

'Now then. Are you sitting down?' Claudia
began.

'Course not. I'm standing on my head.'

'Look. Don't be silly.' Came the immediate
response. 'Take the phone into your lounge and get
comfy. I have news.'

'Darling, I wish you wouldn't be so dramatic.
What sort of news?' Jackie was in no mood for
whatever was about to be sprung on her. She carried
the phone into the lounge; sat down and took a final
swig of the tea she'd been drinking before nodding
off. The tea was stone cold.

'Ugh,' she murmured.

'Don't ugh, until you've heard me out.'

'I'm surprised you heard. It was a bit of a
reaction to some tea I drunk.'

'Ah. You're a bit drunk. Well, not to worry. I
expect you've had a beastly day. *So* unlike mine.
Anyhow, provided you don't have to drive tonight,

do *not* feel guilty, my precious. I'm sure you have earned a little tipple.'

Perfect, thought Claudia. Her lover was most agreeable on the rare occasions she'd seen her tipsy.

Before Jackie could muster up enough enthusiasm to correct her, Claudia continued.

'Listen to this. A light, bright, Cotswold stone cottage with mature exquisite, landscaped gardens. Situated near the popular village of Chipping Norton. The house dates back to...'

Jackie yawned and then groaned.

'There's no need to give me every last detail. What's the rental? And when do you want to go? I'll book a week off. I could do with a break.'

'Rent? And why should we be lining some greedy landlord's pocket with rent?'

Oh-oh. Jackie became instantly alert. What had she been up to?

'Look. I'm shattered. Can we ..?'

'No. Let me finish. Wakey wakey darling. Just a few minutes more. Then you can sleep off the drink.'

'I haven't been..' Jackie began. Thinking she would need a large one. If she didn't find a way to put an end to this ridiculous conversation.

Claudia caried on regardless. Adopting the self-same tone as only hours ago in the agents.

'Dates back to early nineteenth century and is beautifully presented. The property offers open plan living whilst retaining original... do you hear? *Original,* period features. Now listen to this. *Inglenook* fireplace. *And* a wood burner. Are you still there?'

'Mmm.' Jackie murmured; she adored a wood burning fire. Her interest had been kindled.

'Best bit coming up then. For you and your outdoor living.' Jackie also loved the outdoors when not confined to that dreary court building. And Claudia, of course, loved entertaining. She played her ace card. 'Beautifully landscaped gardens offer an enchanting space for outdoor living. She paused only for breath. 'Tailor made for you and I. Meant to be, I'd say.'

How was Jackie going to shut her up if she resisted? She took herself, along with the phone, to the drinks' cabinet. Tucking the receiver under her ear, she poured herself a large gin and tonic. She might well be drunk before the night was out, the way things were going, she thought. Not only fulfilling Claudia's prophecy. But allowing her, as usual, to get her way.

Fifteen minutes later they were still on the phone, discussing the pros and cons of joint property ownership. Along with the possibility of moving in together. Also whether it was time for Jackie to take the retirement she'd been planning. She was more than secure with what Ivan had left which, of course, included his police pension. Plus a lump sum for being killed in the course of duty. Mortgage free, too. With Aunt Flo's legacy settling what had been outstanding. So, Jackie was a woman of means. As was Claudia, whose art sales continued to soar. Her painting had become, not only financially rewarding, but therapeutic. What was more, she'd already been advised by Mr. Stribley, her half share of Parklands would be adequate to purchase Artists' Cottage. So, there was no pressure. The way Claudia's saw things anyhow. She was simply doing Jackie a favor; presenting her with an investment opportunity too good to miss.

Jackie was on her third drink as the protracted debate trundled on.

'How much then? And when's the viewing?'

'Oh, my precious. I *knew* you'd see sense. The asking price is.. er, I've forgotten. But the viewing's when I've phoned Rupert Brookes tomorrow first thing.' Her heart was ready to explode. 'How about Saturday? Can you get up here Friday evening?'

There was a clatter and Jackie realized Claudia had dropped the phone. Then, following a muffled scuffle came 'Whoopee. How exciting. Can you stay Saturday, too? Is there someone to see to that blest dog? Just don't bring it here. But can you stay? Oh, do say yes.'

'OK. Yes. Provided Brenda's on hand to see to Candy. And provided I don't drink myself silly in the meantime. Night night.'

There was a click which Claudia hadn't heard. When, five minutes later, she replaced the receiver. Puzzled by the lack of response to the rest of her rapturous ramblings. Concerning a property she had not set eyes on.

Some people are so rude was going through her mind as she finally put down the phone.
They say you don't know a person till you live with 'em was running through Jackie's.
As she crashed out on the sofa.

# CHAPTER 43

'I don't care who has put an offer in. We'll better it.
Won't we, Jacqueline?'

Claudia stared menacingly at Jackie, then
eyeballed Rupert Brookes with the same air of
defiance which had marked her out, on that first
visit to his office. Brookes had scanned his
appointments book. His initial reaction of, oh no,
it's that bloody woman, turned into intense curiosity
as he sped along ten minutes behind schedule. Who
could be contemplating setting up home at Artists'
Cottage, Howler Lane, with a woman as mad as a
hatter? Perhaps the other party was a little crazy,
too. Or maybe coming in a purely advisory role.
The booking had been made in the name of Elliott
and there had been no mistaking that voice when
Gail Scott, Brookes' colleague, took the call. She'd
written in the diary's margin: your client from last
Monday morning. And then drawn a smiley.

'Why, yes.' Jackie Foster, the other half of this
strange duo spoke now. In a manner intended to
convey buying and selling houses was something
she did all the time. Lest the agent should think they
were a bit green around the gills; two naïve females
with far more money than sense.

Because the fact of the matter was, if Claudia's
impetuosity was not nipped in the bud, they could
be biting off more than they could chew.

'What did you say the others have offered?'
Jackie strove to take control.

Rupert Brookes flicked through his file.

'Ah yes, here we are. A hundred and seventy-one
thousand. Four thousand shy of the asking price.'
He looked from one woman to the other.
'Gentleman from the States and his wife, wanting a
base for exploring our beautiful English
countryside. Cash buyers. Looking to complete
quickly.'

Jackie had driven them down from Parklands,
first thing. Upon arrival, they'd spent a whole half
hour inside the cottage with Claudia dancing
delightedly, from room to room. Almost prancing
upstairs, to a series of 'oh's' and 'ah's' and 'I know
what we can do with this' accompanying her every
step.

Outside, the two women had been left alone for a
short while. They'd just stolen a kiss when Brookes
re-joined them. At which point Jackie made plain
her reservations. The property was delightful. Inside
and out. To accommodate guests or provide lots of
space from each other. Should it prove needed.
With bags of potential to put their own stamp on it,
too. But there was so much more to consider before
putting in any offer. Jackie looked straight at the
agent.

'Many thanks for showing us round. We'll...'

'The whole asking price. I'm having it. Take it
off the market right away.' Claudia cut in.

'B..but..' Jackie was rendered speechless.

'No. I'm phoning Mr. Stribley. He'll get things
moving for me. Whether you're in on the deal.'

Lowering her specs and peering at Jackie over them, she continued 'Or not.'

Jackie once again found her voice and, in perfect Dragons' Den fashion, had no hesitation in declaring herself - well and truly *OUT*. Perhaps, for the first time, in every sense of the word, too. While the agent was forced to await his moment.

'Ladies, I can see you've some serious thinking to do.' He eventually managed to chime in, looking at his watch, all the time edging nearer to his car. His phone became the instrument of redemption. He felt it vibrate in his jacket pocket. 'Excuse me, I must dash,' he said, retrieving the phone, already twenty minutes late for his next appointment. 'You can ring the office Monday when you've had time to talk things over.' He pressed the answer key.

'Hello, Adam. Yes, I know. I'm running late. Tell the Bartram's I'm on my way and give my apologies.' At which Brookes, having locked up the cottage, leapt into his vehicle and sped off.

He had just acquired two promising clients for his young colleague to cut his teeth on, he reflected, keeping his foot down, all the way there. Adam Fielding was a newbie. The Elliott Foster deal was just the thing for Fielding to gain vital experience. In what could be a very cut and thrust business.

What Brookes needed most was the week's leave he hadn't yet taken. And, notwithstanding his late arrival had filled in the necessary form.

Before holding out a hand to Mr. Bartram. With, to his total relief, a sane and sensible looking Mrs. Bartram at his side.

# CHAPTER 44

'What a salesperson. Walking away from a cast iron deal.'

They had hit the road and were just minutes away from the viewing when Claudia began again. On and on she went.

'I was in sales before I married Charles. And it's not the way one does business.'

Jackie might have been a goldfish, the number of times she opened and closed her mouth. Before anything came out.

'You never told me.' She eventually replied.

'Yes, I did.' Claudia turned to give Jackie an indignant stare. The atmosphere was tense. How could her lover pour cold water on, what was to her way of thinking, a done deal?

'What did you sell?' Jackie found herself more and more drawn into conversation, despite the buildup of traffic.

'I was a top sales consultant and chief window dresser for Sangsters Ladies' Outfitters in Shrewsbury, my hometown. I'll have you know. Where else would I have acquired my impeccable flair for fashion?'

They were on the dual carriageway, heading for the motorway.

'You keep your client hot...hot as a flaming poker. When they're as eager to clinch a deal as we are.'

Jackie knew all about being kept hot as a flaming poker. From the early days of their relationship. She took her eyes off the road for no more than a

second, shouting above the roar of the traffic.
'Don't you mean..?'

There was an almighty screech of brakes.
Accompanied by Claudia's shriek of '*watch out.*' A
thunderous bang followed. And then the crunch of
metal. It was the last thing Claudia was to
remember.

The emergency services were there quickly. Jackie,
unhurt but frozen in shock, sat staring ahead for
several minutes, unable to move a muscle. When
she did, dazed and with men in uniforms hovering
about her, they lifted her out of the car. Just as a
burly, middle aged lorry driver was giving his
statement to the police. His lorry had been in the
outer lane. He'd swerved to avoid the little car
which had veered across the white line and into his
path. The front of the lorry had clipped the back end
of the car, sending it into a spin, leaving it facing
the wrong way, on the inside lane of the
carriageway.

The road had been swiftly closed. And Claudia,
still in her seat, was drifting in and out of
consciousness while the fire service worked,
incessantly, to free her trapped legs. Every so often
she would murmur first Jackie's then Charles's
name. An ambulance stood by, ready to transfer her
to the John Radcliffe in Oxford. Soon as she was
released.

Jackie was given a going over on the spot. Quite
miraculously, no physical damage had been done.
Apart from a large bruise on her upper arm where
the airbag had been deployed. So that was

something to give thanks for. The front end of the car had caved in, however, and Claudia's legs had taken a bashing. The paramedics insisted Jackie should go in the ambulance to be properly checked out. A legal requirement they said, and she was happy to comply. Beside herself with anxiety, she needed to stay with Claudia, then arrange to get back to Seaport when, hopefully, Jess and Tristram arrived. The Elliott family members were in the process of being informed.

Meantime, an officer explained to Jackie they'd be taking her car for inspection after the accident scene photographs, checks and reports were completed. She wasn't allowed back inside the vehicle, of course. Much as she longed to comfort Claudia being released from the crumpled metal.

It was turned two when Claudia was stretchered into the waiting ambulance, half conscious and moaning. Every so often she'd whisper, 'Jackie. Where's my Jackie? What happened?'

She had been given various tests as well as morphine for the pain. Jackie got close as possible and shouted, 'It's OK. I'm here.'

The paramedics busied themselves, prodding and poking with their equipment. Asking 'Can you feel this, Claudia? Can you feel that?'

'She's deaf.' Jackie explained. Before, wailing and flashing, the ambulance wound its way through the trail of vehicles at a standstill.

Jackie's last memory of Claudia on that fateful day, a day which had started with such promise, was of her being wheeled away on a hospital trolley, towards theatre.

There was nothing to do but wait. The duty doctor had advised upon her own discharge, once she'd been checked over. The tests and x-rays Claudia was about to undergo would reveal the extent and nature of the injuries which appeared confined to her legs, he explained. The semi-consciousness being due to the shock and the pain she was in, and the drugs administered to alleviate it, he said.

For Jackie, it was a trauma taking place too soon after her widowhood, for her to process. And it was Guy and Laura who eventually arrived at the hospital, to get her back to Seaport and to her job, if she could face it. By a miracle of Grace and by some means of transport, next day.

Jess and Tristram had arrived by teatime. They'd all be contacted, they were told, when there was an update. Along with Carolyn and Brad who Jess and Tristram knew were somewhere in the UK when finally they managed to get them. At six months' pregnant, it wasn't news Tristram relished giving his sister. Charles had, of course, been informed.

Exhausted, Jackie dozed on the journey home. When awake, she became consumed with guilt and too numb to pray, as Guy's BMW sped them down the same route, in the opposite direction, past where the accident had happened.

Why, oh why had she let Claudia distract her? Why hadn't she, being the driver, asked her to save the discussion for later? She couldn't even remember what they were chatting about. Except it was something nonsensical regarding a property they'd been to look at. Well, they weren't meant to have it. That she was more than happy to accept. But surely Claudia was not going to be taken from her. And from her family, as well.

On the face of it, however, Claudia's injuries did not appear life threatening. But it was a knock them and their relationship, not to mention their families, could have done without. This was her final reflection, as they pulled into One Blenheim Drive. And, as Candy, too weak to get up from her bed, but against all odds, still alive, whimpered and drooled her delight. At the sight of Jackie.

Whatever the future held for her and her mistress, she was back, for that moment, where Candy knew for certain, she belonged.

# CHAPTER 45

'Please darling can you pass my pills?'

It was a typical English summer's day. The sun was out one minute. The next, the sky was overcast with every chance of rain.

Jackie got up from her sunbed. Considering her skin tone, she'd managed to acquire a healthy glow, having moved lock, stock, and barrel into Parklands that spring. She took two pills from several types of medication Claudia was on, from their dispenser. She walked over to where her partner sat in her specially adapted garden chair. Claudia, whose numeracy skills would never have landed her a job in the treasury, was grappling with memory issues now, too.

'Here we go.' Jackie put two tablets in a shallow dish on the picnic table, directly in front of Claudia. She kissed the top of her head then stroked her hair, as Claudia tipped a small amount of water from her flask into a plastic tumbler.

What a traumatic few years they had experienced. At the start of the new millennium. First, Jackie's loss followed by the accident meant their carefree lifestyle had been curtailed.

Claudia had remained in hospital a month, after the crash. She'd had three operations to restore the broken bones and fractures to her shattered legs. Once allowed home, Jess had stayed while her mother got used to the crutches. Not being able to ride her scooter ever again had come as the hardest blow of all. The machine stood in its shed and would do so, for as long as she lived. A treasured memento of life on her open-air mode of transport, around the English countryside she knew and loved. The blow had been softened by the purchase of a shiny mobility scooter for outdoors. Then, for around the house, a small wheelchair had been acquired. And a stair lift meant she could sleep upstairs again. Having made do with Charles's old study, at first.

When the Elliott's divorce, along with a financial settlement was reached, it had been, thankfully, without the need to sell Parklands. Seeing Jackie, at having taken retirement, was able to sell Blenheim Drive then buy Charles out. It had set the seal on the women's relationship with Mr. Stribley delighted to execute the conveyance. Early on, with Claudia still in hospital, Jackie had purchased something more practical to replace the written off Millie. A wheelchair friendly affair. In preparation for their new lifestyle.

Candy had been laid to rest, not long after the accident. This was especially sad for Laura who, despite her veterinary training, had been unable to save her. She was buried in the grounds of her and Guy's country home in Hampshire's New Forest. The couple had married soon as Laura completed her qualification and following Guy's promotion to head of department. Laura, having joined a practice a short drive away meant there were few loose ends to tie up.

The following year, as Spring turned into Summer, one especially warm Sunday evening, heading home from church, alongside the canal, Jackie found herself struggling to keep up with Claudia's new mode of transport. Until, both her and it, came to a sudden halt. Claudia was having a similar moment to the one which had prompted her to phone Jackie, at the end of another evening service. A decade and a half ago now.

After applying the brake to her new machine, Claudia clasped Jackie's right hand in both of hers and took an enormous breath.

'Darling. It's time.'

'Time?' Jackie had been instantly worried and checked her watch. 'Oh, it's seven thirty and we forgot to bring your pills, didn't we? Is your tummy bothering you? Come along then. The sooner we get back, the better.'

Claudia dropped Jackie's hand like a hot brick and, whipping off her specs, treated her to one of her fiercest glares.

'Oh, you and your stomach. You eat too quickly. That's your trouble.'

Jackie scowled. 'I never said a thing about *my* tummy. It's fine.'

'You didn't? Then I misheard.' Claudia had replied, apologetically. 'I should have kept my device in till we got home, I expect.'

'What I'm trying to say is, whatever's playing you up, let's not hang about.'

Undeterred, Claudia had clasped Jackie's right hand again in both of hers.

'Well, what *I'm* trying to say is..' she took a great gulp of the evening air and carried on.

'Let's get married.'

Jackie gaped open mouthed. The setting couldn't have been more romantic. And, though, deep down delighted, she had been taken by total surprise and couldn't fathom exactly what Claudia had in mind. It wasn't something they'd discussed. She was, of course, aware of the proposed legislation to allow same-sex civil partnerships. But it wasn't finalized. And, in any event, couldn't see the pair of them taking on the role of trailblazers.

Moving in together had been a major step and Jackie was content. Their joint home ownership and her taking on the role of Claudia's care giver, she had embraced wholeheartedly, as the ultimate act of loyalty and commitment.

Claudia had, nonetheless, kept tight hold of her hand, trying to read every twitch of emotion, to cross her Jackie's face.

'Oh, *please*.'

Letting go of Jackie's hand, she put her own together in an attitude of prayer. Her way of asking the Good Lord's blessing, too, upon her proposal. 'Pretty please. Say you will.' She then went on.

'But.. but we can't. It's not..' Jackie began.

'Well. You know what I mean. Let's do whatever *is* possible and soon as possible, to legalize things between us. You're the expert on that score.'

Claudia had become aware of her limitations. Compared to the relative sprightliness of her partner. There was no way she was willing to risk losing Jackie. Not after all they'd been through. And, once the shock had subsided, Jackie took little persuading.

She had known from the start Claudia was the one. She took Claudia's face in both of her hands and kissed her, smack bang on the lips. Just as a dog walker was approaching. The dog, with a great woof, bounded towards them. As Jackie withdrew the kiss and as Claudia laughed merrily. Not minding a jot, the dog echoing their jubilation.

'Yes, *yes*. A thousand times yes,' Jackie cried. Tears streaming down her face as she began a jolly jig round the stationary carriage. The dog whooped and yelped repeatedly. Before getting called to heel by his owner. And as the women moved off.

Back at Parklands, possible dates, along with venues, guest lists and, quite naturally outfits, were but a handful of topics forming the focal point of a discussion which went on well after midnight.

Over a large gin and tonic for Jackie. With a small drop of red wine, enough to give Claudia the rosiest of glows The kind Jackie had not seen light up her face. For a very long time.

# CHAPTER 46

## A BEAUTIFUL SPRING DAY 2006
## THE CEREMONY

'Here's to the future, you two.' The congratulations poured forth and the champagne bottles began to pop. Soon as Pastor Bill of the Community Church had laid hands of blessing on the couple. At the end of their Civil Partnership Ceremony. And, as Claudia and Jackie joined hands, to gaze adoringly at each other. In the way newlyweds do.

The happy event was being held in a splendidly decked out function room at Kentley Golf Club. Close family members of both sides were present with their significant others. All except Tristram who was touring the Far East before taking up an accountancy post in London. Carolyn and Brad were there with three-year-old Melissa Marie, having come to the end of an extended stay, at an undisclosed venue in the UK.

'Just staying with friends, mummy. So, Brad can clinch a super important deal,' was all Carolyn had been willing to divulge, a twinkle in her eye. At which Claudia's curiosity had been aroused to the extreme. Although since her recovery, she'd become too involved with her artwork to dwell on anything for long. Jess had brought Natasha, her partner of two years. Nattie was chief buyer for a large fashion house in the Midlands. Laura and Guy were, of course, in attendance. With Laura sporting the first signs of a baby bump. They were due a little boy in the autumn.

Laura had never seen Jackie look so radiant as
when she pushed Claudia into the room to the
accompaniment of Jane McDonald's version of *This
is the Moment:*

*This is the moment*
*The final test*
*Destiny beckoned*
*I never reckoned second best*
*This is the day*
*See it sparkle and shine*
*When all I've lived for becomes*
*Mine*

The women's declarations of promise to one
another had just been exchanged when Pastor Bill
read out a *Shelley* poem of Claudia's choosing:

*All love is sweet*
*Given or returned*
*Common as light is love*
*And its familiar voice, wearies not everyday*
*They who inspire it most are fortunate,*
*As I am now.*
*But those who feel it most*
*Are happier still'*

The couple then exchanged rings. Before the
families, along with friends from the Community
church and even a handful from St Cuth's, indulged
in the most sumptuous of spreads, laid on by the
Club's caterers. All except for Claudia's own
version of Coronation Chicken,

A dish which had formed part of her offering to Jackie on that first visit to Parklands. The cake was a lavish four tier affair, decorated with rainbow icing. The club's special functions room had been hired until well into the evening. Meaning the guests were able to dance and party on, to the accompaniment of Moonshine. A four-piece band in which Guy's brother played drums.

What proved the absolute highlight, not only of their special day, but of the year, so far, was Carolyn and Brad's surprise contribution.

The band had just struck up *Save the Last Dance* for Me when Jackie grabbed Claudia by her wrists, insisting they hit the floor. With a supreme effort, she shuffled round, holding tightly onto Jackie. Afterwards flopping into the nearest chair to a massive clap of hands, before a booming voice which was Brad's, requesting a moment of quiet filled the air. As next came an announcement.

'We know you will all want to join Carolyn and myself in wishing this charming pair a long, joy filled and most blessed future. And with this in mind we want to make a presentation.'

Jackie, still on her feet, looked across at Brad who now had their daughter lying fast asleep on his shoulder. While Claudia, having not quite heard what the fuss was about, fixed her gaze upon Carolyn who was holding up a pink envelope. She walked over to her mother and bending to kiss her cheek, and Jackie's too, pressed the small bulky package into Claudia's hand.

Claudia's fingers fumbled to tear it open. When she finally succeeded, it was to reveal two keys on a ring accompanied by a notecard. Jackie bent to look over her partner's shoulder as Claudia began to read out the message. In her own inimitable style.

'Welcome to your anytime holiday home.' Her voice rose to a shriek; she needed a moment then spluttered in a voice not in the least typical of her ladies' tea party one *'Artists Cottage.'* She stared, open mouthed, at Jackie. Too overcome to utter another word; she handed her the keys and the note. Jackie took over, a tremor in her voice.

*'Welcome to your Anytime Holiday Home at Artists' Cottage, 5 Howler Lane, Chipping Norton. Your honeymoon and new life together start here.'*

Claudia summoned every bit of strength she had left, to get up off the chair. As, with the aid of her stick one side and Jackie holding her on the other, she staggered across the room to throw her arms around her daughter and son-in-law. Just as Melissa woke to join the jubilation with Jackie huddling in there too. The rest gathering round with loud cheers and thunderous clapping. At the end of a truly joyous occasion.

Minutes later Claudia, having sunk herself into the comfiest sofa in the room and, now hand in hand with her partner, shared her thoughts.

'So, it was *you two* competing with us in the property stakes that fateful day,' Claudia began. Before her face clouded over. Upon realizing the irony of it all. And, as she reflected how her unstoppable determination had played its part in their misfortunes.

Brad winked and gave a slow affirming nod. A huge beam lighting up his cheery round, slightly inebriated face, as Claudia continued her lament.

'Oh, if *only* you'd said something. I wouldn't have given two hoots about the American gent and his wife who Rupert Brookes informed us had put in their offer. Now, would I?' She then turned to Jackie. 'Oh, darling. If *only* we had known.'

'Sssh.' Brad drawled and put a finger to his lips. 'Never mind the if only's. Once we got the devastating news then learned exactly what had taken you on your journey that Saturday and, happening to be in the UK, intending to surprise you, we got straight back to the agent with the full asking price and told him to take it off the market. So, just...just go on. *Shoo.*' He continued, looking straight at Jackie. 'Go on. Get this old gal of yours moving.'

It was quarter to eight.

'I reckon you can be down there by lunchtime tomorrow if you go now to get some kip. Then load up all you need and get on your way, first thing.'

Carolyn joined in.

'Brad's right, mummy. Those keys belong to you and Jackie forever, you know. We had our fill of enjoyment during your recovery period whenever we could get over. Stay long as you like and come and go, often as you please. Our flight back is early next week. Soon as we've had chance to catch up with daddy and Celine. They're flying to London to meet us tomorrow.'

'Bye Ganma Elit and Bye Ganma Foser.' Melissa waved with both hands to have the last word.

On what had been an extraordinary occasion for each of their families and all their friends. Who had witnessed the end of one era. And quite the beginning of another. In the tale of two women who finally proved:

TRUE LOVE CONQUERS ALL

Printed in Great Britain
by Amazon

16895971R00149